Perspective on Power

A Report to the Energy Policy Project of the Ford Foundation

Perspective on Power

A Study of the Regulation and Pricing of Electric Power

Edward Berlin
Charles J. Cicchetti
William J. Gillen

This study was prepared under a
grant to the Public Interest
Economics Center from the Energy
Project of the Ford Foundation

Ballinger Publishing Company • Cambridge, Mass.
A Subsidiary of J.B. Lippincott Company

Published in the United States of America by Ballinger Publishing Company,
Cambridge, Mass.

Second Printing, 1975

Library of Congress Catalog Card Number: 74-12125

International Standard Book Number: 0-88410-312-9 (hb.)
                                    0-88410-313-7 (pbk.)

Printed in the United States of America

Library of Congress Cataloging in Publication Data
Berlin, Edward.
  Perspective on power: a study of the regulation and pricing of electric power.
  Includes bibliographical references.
  1. Electric utilities—United States—Costs. 2. Electric utilities—United States—
Rates. 3. Power resources—Law and legislation—United States. I. Cicchetti,
Charles J., joint author, II. Gillen, William, joint author. III. Title.
HD9685.U5B47   338.4'3   74-12125
ISBN 0-88410-312-9 (hb.)
ISBN 0-88410-313-7 (pbk.)

Contents

List of Tables and Figures

Tables

Figures

Foreword

In December 1971 the Trustees of the Ford Foundation authorized the organization of the Energy Policy Project. In subsequent decisions the Trustees have approved supporting appropriations to a total of $4 million, which is being spent over a three-year period for a series of studies and reports by responsible authorities in a wide range of fields. The Project Director is S. David Freeman, and the Project has had the continuing advice of a distinguished Advisory Board chaired by Gilbert White.

This analysis of electric utility pricing and regulatory policies, entitled "Perspective on Power," is one of the results of the Project. As Mr. Freeman explains in his Preface, neither the Foundation nor the Project presumes to judge the specific conclusions and recommendations of the authors who prepared this volume. We do commend this report to the public as a serious and responsible analysis which has been subjected to review by a number of qualified readers.

This study, like many others in the Project, deals with a sensitive and difficult question of public policy. Not all of it is easy reading, and not all those we have consulted have agreed with all of it. Nor does it exhaust a subject which is complex, controversial, and partly obscured by gaps in the available data. The matters it addresses are of great and legitimate interest not only to those who are investing heavily in electricity generating and distribution facilities, but also to those who consume electrical energy directly in their homes or places of employment, or indirectly in the goods and services they use. The perspectives of these interested parties are not likely to be identical.

In this last respect the present study reflects tensions which are intrinsic to the whole of the Energy Policy Project—tensions between one set of objectives and another. As the worldwide energy crisis has become evident to us all, we have had many graphic illustrations of such tensions, and there are more ahead. This is what usually happens when a society faces hard choices, all of them carrying costs that are both human and material.

But it is important to understand that there is a fundamental difference between present tension and permanent conflict. The thesis accepted by our Board of Trustees when it authorized the Energy Policy Project was that the very existence of tension, along with the inescapable necessity for hard choices, argued in favor of studies which would be, as far as possible, fair, responsible, carefully reviewed, and dedicated only to the public interest. We do not suppose that we can evoke universal and instantaneous agreement, and still less do we presume that this Project can find all the answers. We do believe that it can make a useful contribution to a reasonable and democratic resolution of these great public questions, one which will serve the general interest of all.

The current study is a clear example of what we aim at. It draws on the most recent work in economic theory, empirical cost and demand studies, and experience in other nations, to reach conclusions about changes in electricity pricing and regulatory policy which, in the thoughtful and considered opinions of the authors, are economically desirable. A wide range of outside experts and organizations reviewed the book; and, although not all of them agreed with all of the analysis and conclusions, we do believe that the authors have treated their hard subject with the respect it deserves. I commend their analysis to the attention of the American public.

McGeorge Bundy
President, Ford Foundation

Authors' Preface

The electric power industry expanded rapidly during the first two-thirds of the Twentieth Century. Increased industrial productivity and changed living standards were taken for granted almost as quickly as they were achieved. The public took even less interest in the power industry itself. The infamous blackout in the Northeast in the winter of 1965—although merely a mechanical problem of great scope—was an omen. The industry was emerging from a time which has been called a "benign cycle" of decreasing costs and lower prices.

New pressures began converging. Existing technology had been pressed nearer to its physical and engineering limits; technological innovation, which had played an important role in reducing the unit costs of electric power, had reached a plateau. The industry's commitment to a new generating technology—nuclear power—did not, as expected, lower costs. Nuclear plants require enormous amounts of money "up front"—that is, the ratio of capital costs to operating costs is much higher for nuclear plants than for fossil fuel plants. As the cost of borrowing money increases, the cost of building increases. Also, nuclear plants have operated with less reliability than was expected. The forced (unanticipated) outage of such units has been particularly costly.

Growing awareness of and concern for the safety of nuclear plants and for their effect on the environment imposed additional higher costs. Efforts to minimize the risk of nuclear accidents and to lessen the environmental damage forced design modifications and costly delays in construction. Whether such concerns are warranted is beyond the scope of this study; however the costs associated with minimizing these risks are all too real.

Fuel costs increased rapidly as the power industry switched from coal to less polluting forms of fuel oil. A switch back to coal by some plants due to the current shortage of fuel oil has brought the further cost of renovating or purchasing previously displaced coal-handling equipment. Fuel oil and natural gas prices, of course, continue to rise.

The inflation which began in the mid 1960s has affected the electric power industry more severely than other sectors of the economy, due to the industry's high ratio of fixed to variable costs. Also, the regulatory practice of tying revenue requirements to historic costs has meant that the replacement and expansion of plants and equipment leads to yet higher prices. Additions to capacity are persistently underpriced, thus spurring the demand for yet more new and costly capacity. The considerable reliance on outside financing has compounded the adverse effect of inflation.

Indeed, the "benign cycle," in which improved efficiency in electric power production offset moderate inflation, ended in the latter part of the 1960s. Revenues continued to increase, but higher costs eroded utilities' earnings. Utility management has had a difficult time reacting to these new pressures while dealing with protests from consumer and environmental groups in rate proceedings.

Consumer groups view the recent rash of rate increases and company claims of rising costs, and say that continuation of promotional practices, quantity discounts (or declining block rate pricing), and lower rates for industrial users are not fair. Environmentalists have also opposed continuation of historic pricing practices, pointing out that even during the period of decreasing costs *all* costs may not have been decreasing. The social (including environmental) costs of power were largely ignored. While cheap in terms of private costs (those costs borne by consumers of electric power), electric power production exacted a greater price from society as a whole.[a] At the same time, greater environmental damage was sustained. Environmentalists urge pricing reform as an alternative to capacity expansion.

Industrial interests, with a considerable financial stake in electric power prices, have also been well represented in rate proceedings, arguing vigorously for the need both to remain cost competitive and to protect jobs. While regulatory commissions have continued to grant rate increases, they have begun to examine the pricing practices of the utilities, and to question the need for proposed new generation and transmission facilities.

Utility management has been compelled by events to balance each competing interest within the confines of the regulatory framework. State legislatures and courts have also become involved in examining industry activities. In short the electric power industry now involves new characters, and a new chorus of protests. We shall attempt to examine the economic, legal, and political dimensions of this new stage and offer a series of intermediate and long run policy recommendations. We will attempt to clear up misunderstandings which have cropped up among industry, environmentalists, economists, and

---

[a]While it is true that virtually everyone in society is also a consumer of electric power, not all consume at the same rate, nor incur the same external costs associated with consumption. It is therefore necessary to make the distinction.

utility commissioners; misunderstandings which in some cases hang on the meanings of words, the use of concepts, or conflicts in priorities.

We first examine rising cost trends to which we have already referred, considering the various uses of the term "economies of scale." Then we discuss briefly the relationship between price and quantity of electricity demanded, which is treated more fully in Appendix A. We review typical rate structures and then discuss economic principles and alternative strategies for pricing, which we postulate will lead to a more efficient allocation of the costs of electricity.

In Chapter Four we give a brief history of the laws which structure the regulation of the industry. Here we emphasize possibilities for improving licensing procedures, rate regulation, and pooling arrangements by better use of existing authority. We also discuss briefly the role of the Atomic Energy Commission and the Securities and Exchange Commission.

We then describe the serious shortcomings of the recommended reforms and outline a proposed reorganization of the regulatory framework. Finally we discuss the possibility of restructuring the industry in line with our proposed regulatory reorganization.

Preface

The Energy Policy Project was initiated by the Ford Foundation in 1971 to explore alternative national energy policies. This book, *Perspective on Power*, is one of the series of studies commissioned by the Project. It is presented here as a carefully prepared contribution by the author to today's public discussion about ratemaking and other regulatory practices in the electric utility industry. It is our hope that each of these special reports will stimulate further thinking and questioning in the specific areas that it addresses.

The special reports are being released as they are completed, rather than delaying their publication until the Energy Policy Project's final report is completed, because I believe they can make a timely contribution to the public discussion of energy policies. At the most, however, each special report deals with only a part of the energy puzzle; our final report, to be published later in 1974, will attempt to integrate these parts into a comprehensible whole, setting forth the energy policy options available to the nation as we see them.

This book, like the others in the series, has been reviewed by scholars and experts in the field not otherwise associated with the Project, in order to be sure that differing points of view were considered. With each book in the series, we offer reviewers the opportunity of having their comments published in an appendix, and one chose to do so with this volume (see page 169).

Perspective on Power is the authors' report to the Ford Foundation's Energy Policy Project and neither the Foundation, its Energy Policy Project, nor the Project's Advisory Board have assumed the role of passing judgment on its contents or conclusions. We will express our views in the Project's final report that will complete this series of publications.

S. David Freeman
Director,
Energy Policy Project

Acknowledgments

To those at the Energy Policy Project who sponsored this work, we are grateful for encouragement, advice, and assistance—and especially patience; particularly S. David Freeman, William Iulo, and Frances Francis.

Several organizations have been important in our direct involvement in these matters, especially the Environmental Defense Fund, and its Executive Committee; and the Public Interest Economics Center and its president, Allen Ferguson. We are indebted to them for their early and continuing encouragement in these activities.

Russel Cherry, Gordon Corey, Paul Davidson, Virginia Duin, Lawrence Edelman, Michael Flynn, Wesley Foell, O. Scott Goldsmith, Lawrence Hammerling, Steven Hanke, Yolanda Holy, Paul Joskow, John L. Jurewitz, Myron Kwast, James Nelson, Margaret Neuer, Hubert Nexon, Charles Olson, Nina Questal, V. Kerry Smith, Eugene Smolensky, Paul Smolensky, Robert Spann, John Stewart, Edward Sullivan, and Leonard Weiss have contributed generously of their time, their criticism, and their good humor. Most of these people would dissent from at least portions of the text that follows, and some of them from virtually all of it; but our work is better because of their contribution and we are grateful.

Carole Grossman assisted us with the final draft, bringing order to the disorder that results from three minds trying to come together as one. To the extent that elements of obtuseness or dishevelment lurk still in these pages, it is because we—and not she—had the last crack at it.

To Marilyn, Brenda, Douglas, Patricia, Colleen, Skippy, and Carol—it always seems that it is vastly insufficient simply to express gratitude for and to acknowledge their contributions and sacrifice, and so it seems now.

Edward Berlin
Charles Cicchetti
William Gillen

Washington, D.C.   1974

Principle Policy
Recommendations

I. *Tariff Design: The Imperative of Peak Load Pricing*

At present electricity is marketed in the United States under rate tariffs which discriminate, first, among the *uses* to which the electricity will be put and second, by the *volume* consumed. Typically the residential and small commercial customer receives a lower unit cost when he increases his overall level of consumption during the billing period. The large commercial and industrial customer achieves similar unit reductions through increased consumption; the two-part tariff is a further inducement to maintain a uniform level of demand or high load factor.

Tariffs rarely give consideration to the *time* of consumption over the daily cycle. This failing represents a critical defect for it costs the utility, and society, far more to serve a load which is demanded at the time of system peak than it would to serve an equivalent (or greatly increased) load off-peak. It requires building capacity adequate to serve peak demands, putting into service the most inefficient, most fuel consumptive, and therefore most environmentally damaging units at the time of system peak.

As weather-sensitive loads contribute increasingly to peaks, it becomes imperative to offer consumers inducements to shift loads off-peak. Tariff designs must focus on the improvement of *system* load factor, not on the improvement of *individual* load factor.

The appropriate solution is peak load or time-of-day pricing. Such tariffs would be cost-based and would charge each customer the full marginal cost associated with a particular service at the time it is demanded. Prices based on the full recovery of marginal cost would avoid cross-subsidization among consumers, end reliance on irrelevant and discriminatory consumer characterizations, achieve equity, encourage the efficient use of capacity and fuels, and promote rate stability. It would further provide an appropriate set of cost-based incentives to each customer; when use patterns change, revenues and costs will change in a direct relationship with one another.

Time-of-day pricing for electricity should be applied according to the expected net benefits; that is, the capital and fuel consumption savings to be expected, less the added cost of metering by time-of-day. In the case of relatively large industrial loads, where recording demand meters are already in place, the new pricing system will involve little or no additional metering cost. For other large volume consumers, metering will be a relatively small portion of the total costs, and therefore not a significant obstacle to time-of-day tariffs.

In the case of residential and small commercial consumers, metering costs would be relatively more significant, but this must be weighed against the propensity of these consumers to contribute disproportionately to expensive seasonal peak demands such as air conditioning loads. Accordingly, time-of-day pricing for small users might proceed on an optional basis, with consumers bearing the additional metering cost in exchange for the opportunity to reduce their electric bills. Alternatively, surveys could be undertaken to estimate consumer responsiveness and the appropriate extent of time-of-day pricing.

II. *The Inclusion of Externalities in Tariffs*

The generation, transmission and distribution of electricity impose real costs upon society—the so-called "externalities" which are not reflected in utility financial statements. To the extent that consumer prices recover only the utility's costs of supplying power, the user is in fact being subsidized by society at large or by that portion of society shouldering the external costs. Although it is difficult to estimate social costs accurately, it is inappropriate to continue to assign a zero value to external costs. Prices should reflect the full cost of service whether those costs are borne by the utility or by society.

Utilities must not be permitted, however, to charge these higher prices unless they actually use their increased revenues to reduce the environmental damage associated with providing electricity.

We recommend the creation of area-wide externality funds—administrative bodies charged with participating in rate proceedings, to urge the inclusion of sufficient funds to compensate for external costs. These revenues would be paid directly into the externality funds, which would then be responsible for spending them in the way best designed to compensate society for the amenity lost or social cost incurred.

III. *Interim Leadership at the Federal Level*

The Federal Power Commission, making full use of its authority over wholesale prices, should move to implement pricing policies that would promote economic and social efficiency and secure open, comprehensive, regional coordination. Without leadership at the federal level it is most unlikely that needed changes will be undertaken on a broad basis at the state level.

It is essential that the FPC, making use of its resources and ability to undertake nationwide economic analyses, develop the data base necessary for basic tariff design reform. The states could participate through a joint-board procedure. Consideration of a time-of-day tariff experiment should be given high priority.

Further, in view of the economic, environmental and social waste—as well as the anti-competitive implications—inherent in power supply planning mechanisms that do not include the full participation of all utilities within a region, the FPC must utilize its ample authority to effect more appropriate industry cooperative arrangements.

IV. *Early Disclosure of Utility Plans*

Utilities should disclose power supply plans at least two years before filing an application seeking site approval. If citizen interventions have delayed needed capacity expansions, it is in large part because utility planners have been unwilling to let the public into the planning process before proposals are in their final stages. The siting of generation and transmission facilities has a profound impact on local planning objectives. The public has a right to be heard before options are foreclosed. We suggest that the entire process would be expedited if each certifying agency required applicants to submit, two years in advance of filing a complete application, a "skeletal" filing disclosing the location, type and size of the planned capacity addition. During that period the abbreviated filing should be made available to all interested individuals and public officials, and circulated to all utilities within the region, to assure that the proposal is best designed to avoid unnecessary duplications.

V. *An Ultimate Regulatory Restructuring*

Serious consideration should be given to shifting the focus of the regulatory commissions. It is now apparent that to achieve the desired level of efficiency, utility operations must be closely integrated on a regional level. Regional regulatory commissions—enjoying supervisory responsibility over both siting and rate determinations—could help to assure that power supply plans are developed and implemented according to the schedule and format that best serves overall regional interests while still preserving and promoting competitive diversity. The public could then address the underlying policy issues, rates of growth, generation mix, etc., now ignored in siting and tariff proceedings, by examining them in a time frame in which trade-offs can be balanced.

VI. *The Restructuring of Industry*

Serious consideration should be given to separating the generation and transmission of electricity from the distribution function. Many of the historical justifications for complete vertical integration of electric utility functions are no longer applicable. Those that remain may be more than offset by anti-competitive implications and issues of economic and social efficiency.

The establishment of a limited number of bulk power suppliers within each region could improve financing, coordination and competition. Moreover, this separation of function could help make state regulation over distribution activities more effective and serve to make the management of what is essentially a service industry more responsive to local objectives.

Perspective on Power

Chapter One

Recent Cost Trends

It has been generally observed that average total costs in the electric power industry have been rising in recent years.[a] Both capital (fixed) costs and production (variable) costs have contributed to this increase, although production costs represent a much smaller proportion of the total. Approximately 80 percent of production costs are fuel costs;[b] and regulatory commissions have increasingly tended to permit the flow-through of higher fuel costs in the form of "fuel adjustment clauses" without requiring extensive and expensive rate proceedings.

There is, to be sure, some undesirable weakening of the competitive vigor of the fuel-purchasing utility when additional fuel costs may thus be easily recovered. But since fuel costs are readily identifiable and accountable (they do not require complex and esoteric accounting as other items may), from the standpoint of the utility—if not the consumer—simple fuel cost adjustment is preferred to formal rate proceedings. The extraordinary leap of fuel prices, especially during the winter of 1974, will of course be a continuing, perhaps worsening, burden for consumers for years to come. This does not diminish the awesome prospect of the electric power industry's trying to raise hundreds of billions of dollars in coming years in order to finance capacity expansion. We are inclined to believe that the cost of additional capacity will continue to dominate rate proceedings. It is the fundamental and persistent reason why the price of electricity can be expected to rise.

[a]See, for example, K.D. Roe and W.H. Young, "Trends in Capital Costs of Generating Plants," *Power Engineering* (June 1972): 40; "Plant Capital Costs Spiraling Upward," *Electric World* (July 1, 1971): 36; W.R. Steur, "Increasing Power Plant Costs in the 1970's," *Public Utilities Fortnightly* (February 4, 1971): 29; and "18th Steam Station Cost Survey," *Electrical World* (November 1973).

[b]See, *Steam Electric Plant Construction Cost and Annual Production Expenses*, 24th Annual Supplement—1971, Federal Power Commission, Table 8. To be sure, future supplements will show a significant increase in this statistic.

Historically, the unit costs of adding to utility plant and capacity have been less than the average cost of plants already on line. That no longer appears to be the case, whether the costs are expressed in real or nominal terms. Figure 1-1 indicates the ten-year rise in an index of public utility construction costs and the corresponding lower rate of increase in the wholesale price index.

Such cost trends provide an illustrative starting point for closer analysis. Costs of the electric power industry depend upon the interaction of many factors, the four most important of which are the following:

1. Rising absolute and relative factor prices.
2. Technical change.
3. More stringent environmental and safety requirements.
4. Economies of scale.

RISING FACTOR PRICES

In analyzing changes in industry costs it is important to distinguish between rising absolute factor prices (inflation) and changing relative (real) prices. To the

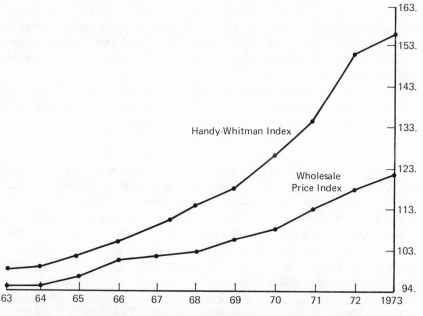

Source: 1) Handy-Whitman Index of Public Utility Construction Costs, *Statistical Yearbook of the Electric Utility Industry, 1972*, Edison Electric Institute, Table B25. 2) *Economic Report of the President, 1973*, Council of Economic Advisors, Washington, D.C., Table C-48.

Figure 1-1. Cost Trends for Public Utilities Compared with the Wholesale Price Index Over a Ten-Year Period (1963-1973)

extent that one is interested in resource allocation or economic efficiency, relative price changes should be the main concern. However, it should be noted that the impact of inflation on a regulated firm differs from that on an unregulated firm, since all costs are not automatically recouped.

The factor inputs of electric utilities can be divided into three categories: capital, fuel, and labor. Capital costs consist of asset prices, such as equipment and materials, and periodic costs such as interest. Other things being equal, an increase in interest rates will have a greater impact on more capital-intensive industries than on less capital-intensive industries. Increases in such costs as field construction labor, coupled with higher quality and safety standards, have greater impacts on industries such as electric power than they do on industries which depend relatively less on these factors.

The soaring cost of construction labor has been a significant factor in the rising cost of new generating plants. In the five-year period from 1962 to 1967 the average annual wage increase in the construction industry ranged between three and six percent. However, in 1969-1970, the average annual increase rose to more than 15 percent, and many wage settlements contained increases of more than 20 percent per year.[c] In 1971 the average annual rate of increase reached 17 percent. Thus total field labor (construction) costs have increased from about 20 percent of total construction costs in the mid 1960s to about 30 percent by 1971. Also, construction delays and the liberal use of overtime significantly add to construction costs. The regulatory commissions' generous attitude toward utilities' interest payments during construction also has pushed consumer costs upward.

Probably the most significant reason for the rising cost of new capacity is the cost of money. Financing terms for utilities have worsened. One indication of this trend is the annual yield on the 40 bonds that comprise the Moody's Public Utility Bond Average. Bond yields were relatively stable during the first half of the 1960s at about 4.6 percent. However, they then increased, and by December 1973 bond yields exceeded eight percent (see Table 1-1). The trend for other corporate securities is similar, but the increase is more significant for the electric utilities than for most other borrowers since utilities (1) are expanding rapidly and with less discretion than other sectors, and (2) tend to require more capital investment per dollar of sales or unit of output. In the next few years the electric utilities will require and have to compete for an even larger share of the available supply of investment funds—and almost certainly will find higher rates than they have previously paid.[d] If the earnings erosion that presently characterizes much of the industry continues, leading to so-called "make whole" rate cases, investors may regard utilities as more risky investments, thus compounding the problem of financing.

---

[c]K.A. Roe and W.H. Young, "Trends in Capital Costs of Generating Plants," *Power Engineering* (June 1972).

[d]"The Utility Bond Bind," *The Wall Street Journal*, July 24, 1973.

Table 1-1.   Average Yield on Utility Bonds

Year	Yield in Percent
December 1965	4.85
December 1966	5.63
December 1967	6.56
December 1968	6.85
December 1969	8.57
December 1970	8.29
December 1971	7.87
December 1972	7.48
December 1973	8.14

Source: Moody's Investors Service, reported in *Statistical Yearbook*, Edison Electric Institute, 65.

TECHNICAL CHANGE

In past decades technical change has had an important effect on the power industry's generating costs. Evidence of this can be seen in the dramatically declining heat rates[e] of electric power plants in the immediate postwar years. However, during the 1960s the heat rates of new fossil fuel power plants remained virtually constant, and in some cases have been increased to assure greater reliability. Technology in the industry was not stagnant, however; in fact during the 1960s one profoundly different production technique was coming into use—nuclear generation.

New production techniques are normally introduced to achieve lower total unit costs. However, the short run impact may be less than expected or may even lead to increased costs. This is especially true when there are unforeseen difficulties and when "learning by doing" is a significant development cost. Such factors appear to be present for nuclear plants. Eight years ago it was generally believed that a large light-water reactor could be built for about $125/KW. The plants begun then are now nearing completion and the actual costs are estimated to be closer to $400/KW. This great increase over planned costs is not due merely to inflation.

Perhaps this represents an overly pessimistic view. To be sure, one lesson of the past several generations is that technological gains often exceed our expectations—even our imaginations. Perhaps there is some ingenious idea, lurking just beyond the periphery of our limited vision, that will soon make

[e]Heat rate is a measure of generating station thermal efficiency, generally expressed in BTU per net kilowatt hour. More specifically, it is total BTU content of fuel burned or of heat released from a nuclear reactor per net kilowatt hour generation. Higher heat rates imply lesser economy of fuel use and greater reliability. The opposite is true for lower heat rates.

these concerns seem trivial. The point, though, is that it may not be wise to presume and act as if it will be so.

A recent analysis by Roe and Young concluded that several factors contributed to these unprecedented cost overruns: (1) The allowance for inflation was too low; (2) the stretching out of construction schedules led to higher costs for interest during construction; (3) most of the schedule stretchout before 1971 occurred after construction had begun; (4) field labor or construction costs were adversely affected by extended construction time as well as by increases in the scope of the work; and finally (5) additional safety measures, unanticipated regulatory proceedings, additional environmental tests and increases in equipment prices all contributed to cost increases.

Some of these costs, such as environmental and safety expenditures, are likely to stay at these higher levels, and perhaps even increase. On the other hand, some of these cost increases are probably due to the experimental nature of this new technology. In retrospect it is probably true that speaking strictly from an economic standpoint, some nuclear plants should not have been constructed in the manner and under the conditions in which they were.

STRINGENT ENVIRONMENTAL AND SAFETY REQUIREMENTS

Although electricity is a clean form of energy at the point of consumption, the generation of electricity typically causes environmental pollution. Fossil fueled plants release sulfur oxides, nitrogen oxides, and particulates into the air, while nuclear plants emit low level radiation. Both types of plants may require more than 120 billion gallons of water each day for cooling, and often discharge large amounts of heated water into lakes and rivers.[f]

During the past decade, federal and state governments have begun imposing air and water quality standards and plant siting restrictions on the industry in an effort to reduce various forms of pollution. Current standards require limitations on the discharge of thermal pollution into natural bodies of water, and reductions in particulate matter, sulfur oxides, and radioactive emissions. It is estimated that equipment needed to meet these standards may add about $25 to $50 per KW for large plants on sites which pose only moderate problems.[g] As technology improves and pollution abates, the unit cost of such equipment may decline. Both the correction of existing pollution and efforts to foresee environmental problems have increased production costs.

Licensing proceedings have expanded in time, and scope. Now even after sites are agreed upon, original construction plans may have to be altered to

---

[f]For a detailed discussion of pollution, see Neil Fabricant and Robert Hallman, *Toward a Rational Energy Policy: Energy, Politics and Pollution* (George Braziller, 1971), p. 15.

[g]Roe and Young, *op. cit.*

take environmental requirements into account. The extent of these alterations varies, depending upon the size and location of the plant. Changes in licensing proceedings have increased personnel needs and caused costly delays in scheduling.

Implications of these cost considerations are necessarily speculative since requirements are still being refined. However, new environmental standards can only push up the costs of an expanding electric system.

ECONOMIES OF SCALE

Definitions

Economies of scale have traditionally been an important aspect of the electric utility industry. Indeed, they constitute one of the principal historic rationales for consciously restricting competition within the industry. However, this concept has been one of the most misunderstood and abused terms in policy discussions. In economic theory, the term "economies of scale" has a very narrow and precise meaning in reference to electric power production: relatively larger production facilities have lower unit costs than relatively smaller facilities.[h] Economies of scale may exist for any of the several phases of power production, e.g., generation, transmission, or distribution. Note especially that economy of scale is defined *for a particular point in time*, which means a given level of technological development and a given set of prices for the various factors of production. Thus, in reference to generation, we would say that economies of scale exist if, for example, a 600 megawatt plant built today had lower unit costs of production than a 400 megawatt plant also built today.

The industry definition is much broader. It includes the economist's definition, but is also used to describe other instances of decreasing costs. There are three ways in which costs may be said to be decreasing and thus three situations which the industry refers to as economies of scale.

1. Short-run decreasing average costs (SRDAC) refers to the costs of production for a plant with a given productive capacity at a particular time. Once the investment in the plant is made, the average cost of higher levels of output declines. This is somewhat analogous to the familiar case of "spreading the overhead." Since electric power requires considerable fixed costs for most phases of its operation, there are numerous instances of short-run decreasing average costs.

2. Long-run decreasing costs (LRDC) fits the economist's definition of economies of scale. Here, plant size is not fixed, and the comparison is between the average production costs of plants of various capacity. It is generally agreed that LRDC typifies the electric power industry in most of its phases.

---

[h]For simplicity in this discussion, our reference here is to average rather than marginal costs. The crucial distinction will be made later.

3. The third notion of decreasing costs admits time to the definition, which means that technical change as well as changes in the costs of the factors of production may be considered. For example, costs could be decreasing if, due to an engineering refinement, the average costs of production are less for a plant of given size today than for a plant of the same size previously. While technological change has been most significant throughout the industry's history, it is questionable whether further breakthroughs are likely in the near future.

Why make these distinctions? Because the best pricing policy for a firm or industry will depend on a particular set of circumstances. Since "decreasing costs" may describe a number of circumstances, there are a number of "best" pricing policies depending on the particular meaning implied by decreasing costs. What is appropriate under one definition may not be under another. Also, while economists limit economies of scale to the second definition, it may mean any or all of these things when used in the parlance of the industry.

A further difficulty arises because some economists observe (irrelevantly, it turns out) that in situations with economies of scale (their own definition), marginal cost pricing will result in a deficit of revenues. The electric power industry is widely observed to exhibit such decreasing costs. The point is illustrated in Figure 1-2. LRAC is the long-run average cost of producing various levels of output (Q). LRMC is the long-run marginal cost of corresponding levels of output. LRMC and LRAC are precisely related, in that any LRAC curve has its own corresponding LRMC, or vice versa.[i] Economists argue that for efficiency reasons, output should be priced at the level of LRMC. For the quantity of output (Q_1), that means price (P_{MC}). The total revenues which would result are, therefore, equal to the rectangle $P_{MC}AQ_1O$. Total costs, however, will be equal to average cost times the quantity produced, or the area of the rectangles $P_{AC}BQ_1O$. Obviously, total costs exceed total revenues, and the enterprise would appear to operate at a loss. At this point economists do not abandon the concept of marginal cost pricing, but nearly everyone else does. This is a matter of needless confusion since the assumed "losses" exist only because of the manner in which costs are defined. In the real world of profits and regulatory proceedings, a loss exists only when revenues fail to equal (or at least approach) a specified level. That level is a function of historic or sunk costs—i.e., costs that represent investment in plant at some previous time when a quite different set of LRAC and LRMC may have existed (recall that LRAC and LRMC are defined for a specific time).

Thus, when an economist speaks of a loss, in this case he is comparing a level of revenues with a level of costs that would be relevant if the system either had no history or was being built from scratch. Noneconomists

---

[i]The reader may refer to any introductory text in economics for a fuller explanation of these terms.

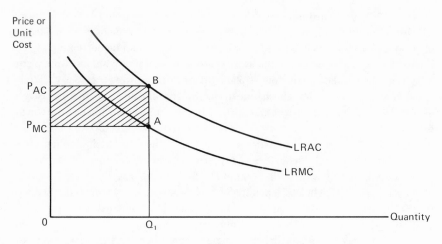

Figure 1-2. Decreasing Costs at a Point in Time

would compare current revenues with the cost of the system as it actually exists—a mixture of facilities new and old and variously depreciated. In sum, no meaningful *a priori* statement can be made respecting the adequacy of revenues and the existence of economies of scale as defined by economists.[j] Nevertheless, the following discussion employs the economists' definition of economies of scale, that is, long-run decreasing costs.

Economies of Scale

There have been several econometric analyses of economies of scale in the electric power industry,[k] dealing primarily with generation, not with transmission and distribution. Many are out of date since data used do not extend beyond 1950; some have been criticized on methodological grounds. Nevertheless, all analyses confirmed the existence of economies of scale at least up to a given size firm.

---

[j]For further clarification and discussion of these points see R. Turvey, *Optimal Pricing and Investment in Electricity Supply*, Cambridge, Massachusetts: The MIT Press, 1968, (See Chapter 4, pp. 58 and 59.)

[k]J. Johnston, *Statistical Cost Analysis*, New York: McGraw-Hill, 1960, pp. 47-73; M. Nerlove, "Returns to Scale in Electricity Supply," *Measurement in Economics* (ed. Carl Christ, et al.), Stanford, Calif.: University Press, 1963, pp. 167-198; Komiya, "Technical Progress and the Production Function in the U.S. Steam Power Industry," *Review of Economics and Statistics* XLIV (May 1962): 156-166; Barzel, "Productivity in the Electric Power Industry," *Review of Economics and Statistics* XLV (November 1963): 401-403; Dhrymes, P. and Kurz, "Technology and Scale in Electric Generation," *Econometrica* XXXII (June 1964): 287-315; W. Iulo, *Electric Utilities—Costs and Performance*, Pullman, Wash.: Washington State University, School of Economics and Business, 1961, pp. 102-107.

There is general agreement that up to about 600 MW, larger generating units will have lower costs (capital, operating, or both) per unit of installed capacity (KW) than smaller units. However, for units above the 600 MW level there is uncertainty. A major source of scale economies up to the 600 MW size results from improved heat rates, which lead to greater engineering efficiency. However, in recent years heat rates in larger plants have sometimes been changed by designers in order to improve reliability—i.e., to avoid unplanned or forced outages. Significant improvement in heat rates for thermal plants beyond present size is not likely.

Additional reasons why there is a threshold beyond which the largest plants may lose a unit cost advantage over smaller plants were cited by Boone[1] as: (1) the effect of the size of plant on reserve requirements; (2) higher forced outage rates for larger plants; and (3) extended maintenance requirements for larger plants.

1. The effect of unit size on reserve requirements is a rather straightforward problem. The contingency to be guarded against is that a particular unit will not be available when needed. If generating capacity consists of a large number of small units, risk is spread over each of those units. If, on the other hand, the generating system was composed of only a few large units, the risk is more concentrated, and the effect of any one of them being unavailable is more significant. Obviously, all other things being equal, a small generating system that relies on a few large generating units carries a heavier burden in terms of capital committed to reserve capacity than the same size system with many smaller units. However, it is not likely that this consideration alone lends any considerable cost advantage to smaller units. Rather, it is the compounded effect of higher absolute reserve requirements together with forced outage and longer maintenance periods which takes the clear edge away from larger units.

2. The forced outage rate for fossil-fueled plants over 600 MW is more than twice that of plants below 600 MW. In this same respect nuclear plants perform worse than fossil-fueled plants.[m]

3. In addition, new plants present more complex maintenance problems than older plants. The average unavailability of the 20 newest stations in a recent *Electric World* survey was placed at 18.6 percent, which was up from 11.3 percent in the previous survey.[n]

Problems with nuclear reactors become particularly acute as they

[1]C.C. Boone, "The Financial Impact of Outages," Paper presented at the 31st Annual Meeting of the American Power Conference, April 1969.

[m]"Report on Equipment Availability for the Twelve Year Period 1960-1971," *Edison Electric Institute* (November 1971): 12.

[n]"17th Steam Station Cost Survey," *Electrical World* (November 1971).

provide an increasing share of new and planned generating capacity. Louis H. Roddis, Jr., President of Consolidated Edison, noted recently that the average availability factor for domestic reactors was 60.9 percent. This contrasts sharply with the 80 percent availability factor usually assumed for new plants.[o] The general point of his remarks was that nuclear generation of electrical power has not lived up to earlier high expectations, and that a major contributing cause has been higher than anticipated forced outage rates.

Philip Sporn,[p] former President of American Electric Power Co., has also discussed the forced outage problem recently. He stated that

> ... [w]ith the growth of atomic power which will take place between now and 1980 no atomic plant can, except for the shortest time, be expected to operate at a capacity factor as high as 80 percent and that, therefore, a more rational capacity factor is ... 75 percent.

Roddis has also testified that as a result of high outage rates, the electric utility industry generally would remain on a size plateau for the foreseeable future "until we have digested the big leap forward." Con Ed's own plants to be built before 1985 would not likely exceed 800 MW for fossil fuel units or 1100 MW for nuclear units.[q]

An analysis of the 1972 reports filed by every major U.S. utility with the Federal Power Commission on the size of planned generating units confirms Roddis's analysis of leveling out in plant size. Fossil fuel units will probably be no larger than 1300 MW—and in most instances less than 1000 MW. Nuclear units will probably not exceed 1250 MW—and most will be smaller.[r] This represents a cutback from previous plans. All large systems and power pools capable of building larger units no longer seem to be planning to do so.

The transmission and distribution aspects of electric power consumption are also said to exhibit substantial economies of scale. Yet, here also there is a need to define terms carefully. Using the static definition, it is certainly true that it costs less on average to transmit ten kilowatts one mile than it does to transmit five kilowatts one mile along the same corridor, although there are thresholds at higher voltages that limit the capacity of any transmission line. Whatever economies of scale there may be, the range is not infinite,

---

[o]Louis H. Roddis, Jr. "Address to the 1972 Atomic Industrial Forum."

[p]Philip Sporn, "Developments in Nuclear Power Economies, January, 1968-December, 1969," A Report to the Joint Committee on Atomic Energy.

[q]Louis H. Roddis, Jr. *Security and Exchange Commission*, File No. 3-1476: In the Matter of the American Electric Power-Columbus Southern Merger, Tr. 12474 and 12471.

[r]See "New Generating Plants: A Summary of Electric Utility Construction Plans 1972-85," *Power Engineering* (April 1972).

although the magnitude of the cost savings associated with higher voltage transmission is substantial up to the limit of engineering feasibility.[s] From another perspective, it may or may not be the case that distribution costs decline as the geographical range of the network expands. It tends to be true that unit distribution costs decline as density of population increases, but this is not always the case.

Perhaps the most common notion of "economies of scale" in transmission and distribution is derived from lower costs associated with greater density of use. This, too, is an instance of "spreading the overhead" and is not a case of true economies of scale.

Finally, no unambiguous and generally applicable statement may be made about the comparative costs of existing transmission and distribution facilities and additions to those facilities.

[s]See, for example, "Considerations Affecting Steam Power Plant Site Selection," Energy Policy Staff, Office of Science and Technology, 1968.

Chapter Two

Pricing: Its Relevance

Recent statistical evidence suggests that price is a most important determinant of the quantity of electricity demanded. The econometric studies on this subject are discussed in Appendix A. Elasticity is the economic term which describes the sensitivity or responsiveness of electricity consumption to changes in price. Elasticity is defined as the ratio of the percentage change in quantity demanded to the percentage change in price. If the coefficient is one,[a] a change in price produces a directly proportional change in quantity demanded. The upper limit of elasticity is infinity.

It has been argued, both in regulatory proceedings and in the trade press, that at least residential demand for electricity is basically insensitive to price; that is, that elasticity approaches zero. There is no current econometric work to support this conclusion. Instead, the argument is based on intuitive grounds. An example often cited is that on hot days, consumers would not turn off air conditioners, even if prices were somewhat higher. They would simply pay the price. Similarly, consumers will light their homes almost without regard for the price.

But such examples miss the point of elasticity. The consumer's decision with respect to any purchase is made, in the jargon of economics, "at the margin," which in this context means that the decision is not whether there will be light or dark, hot rooms or cool, but whether there will be a little more or a little less light, or cool air, or electricity consumption. Thermostats may be turned down as well as off. Or, a modest increase in the price of electricity may justify the cost of added insulation or the selection of a more electricity-efficient appliance.

---

[a]If the coefficient of elasticity is exactly one (actually minus one (−1) but the sign is generally ignored), demand is termed "unit elasticity". If the coefficient is greater (less) than one, demand is termed "elastic" ("inelastic"). Note that "inelastic" does not mean absolute insensitivity of quantity demanded to price; it means rather a sensitivity or responsiveness that is less than proportional to a change in price.

In some instances the elasticity of demand for one commodity will be reflected in the substitution of another energy source, say gas, for electricity. In other cases, a price increase will induce greater economy of use rather than substitution. While generalizations are not always useful, the point is that there is no *a priori* reason to believe that electricity is not price sensitive.

Consider Figure 2-1, which shows the relation between per capita consumption and the average price of electricity to residential users. While econometric studies refine the measurement of the price elasticity coefficient, the simple fact of association is demonstrated in the national averages. In order to understand the importance of pricing, it is necessary to review the pricing practices of the electric utilities, stressing the incentives given consumers, and the effect of those incentives on patterns of consumption.

TYPICAL RATE STRUCTURES

The price charged for a unit of electric power depends on who the customer is, and, for some customers, how much he consumes at one time. Such price

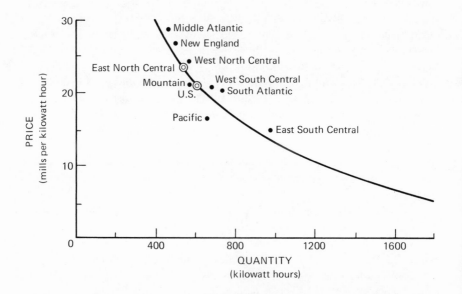

Source: Edison Electric Institute Statistical Yearbook of the Electric Utility Industry for 1971, as represented in "Impact Study of BPA Proposed Rates Increases," Bonneville Power Administration, U.S. Department of the Interior, November 1973.

Figure 2-1. Monthly Residential Demand for Electricity, by Regions, 1971

discrimination is possible only when (1) there is a monopoly or near monopoly, (2) total demand can be divided into separate markets according to the price elasticity of demand in each market, and (3) resales between markets can be prevented.[b]

The first determinant of price, then, is class of customer. The major classification makes distinctions between residential, commercial, and industrial purchasers. Subcategories are also defined, such as residential water heating, municipal street lighting and industrial standby service. There are separate price schedules for each class and subclass. The class distinctions are generally straightforward, although as in tax law some rather peculiar classes are defined for special purposes, occasionally for a particular customer.

The division of customers into classes is, in a literal sense, discrimination. What limits the utility's discretion to make classifications? That is, when, in its division of customers does a utility practice undue discrimination? Discrimination becomes "undue" when there is no reasonable basis for a classification or when rates charged one class of customers do not bear a reasonable relationship to the rates charged another group of customers. Classic discrimination exists where one customer or class of customers is charged a higher price than another for the identical product or service. However, unjust discrimination may also result from charging equal rates for services which warrant different ones.[c] Generally a utility must charge the same rate for the same service to customers similarly situated.[d] Exceptions are usually statutory, and involve charitable institutions, schools, or hospitals.[e] To insure that other classes will not be unduly burdened, preferential rates must collect, at a minimum, the out-of-pocket cost of supplying the particular service.

When a customer uses electricity in such a way as to provide economies to the utility, rate discounts are appropriate and highly desirable. One example would be the case of interruptible service. A customer so served is on notice that his service might be curtailed at any time (for example, when the utility is approaching its period of peak demand). Since the utility need not consider that customer's interruptible load in building capacity for a projected

---

[b]G.J. Stigler, *The Theory of Price*, New York: Macmillan, 1947, p. 223.

[c]See *Payne v. Washington Metropolitan Area Transit Comm.*, 415 F.2d 901, 916 (CA DC, 1968), and authorities cited therein.

[d]*New York Telephone Co. v. Siegal-Cooper Co.*, 202 N.Y. 502, 96 N.E. 109, 111 (1911); *Lazarus & Co. v. Public Utilities Commission*, 7 PUR3d 313, 317, 122 N.E. 2d 783 (Ohio C. Ct., 1954); *Re New England Telephone and Telegraph Company*, 89 PUR3d 417, 422 (R.I., 1971). The FPC has reached a somewhat similar conclusion. See *Cleveland and Akron v. Hope Natural Gas Co.*, 44 PUR(NS) 1, 37 (FPC, 1942), reversed on other grounds in *FPC v. Hope Natural Gas Co.*, 320 U.S. 591 (1944), and *Re Otter Tail Power Co.*, 33 PUR (NS) 257, 263.

[e]See for example, *Washington Rev. Code*, 80.28,080; *Dept. of Public Works v. West Coast Power Co.*, 5 PUR(NS) 204 (Wash., 1934). Where the statute is silent preference has been tested by reference to the overall public benefit derived. Compare *Staten Island Edison Corp. v. N.Y. City Housing Authority*, 61 PUR(NS) 253, 58 U.Y.S. 2d 427 (D.Ct., App. Div., 1945) and *Re Consolidated Edison Co.* (Case No. 14279, July 25, 1951, where preferential rates to hospitals were eliminated).

system peak, rate discounts are appropriate.[f] It is not yet resolved whether rate structures may distinguish among the uses[g] for which electricity is consumed or among existing and new customers.[h]

It may generally be concluded, therefore, that rate differentials are lawful if predicated on a "reasonable" classification scheme. Clearly classifications that are cost based, or predicated on differences in operating conditions, may be sustained if the rate differentials are commensurate with the benefits or detriments thereby achieved. But it must be emphasized that the proponent of a rate differential (customer classification) has the burden of proving that it is in fact predicated on a reasonable foundation.[i]

Rate Structure

Within classes, rates are usually a decreasing step function of the amount of power used. Table 2-1 is an illustrative schedule that might apply to a residential consumer.

For larger, nonresidential users a further distinction is usually made regarding the maximum amount of power consumed at one time. For this purpose, price is separated into the energy component (kwh) and the demand component (KW), both of which are usually decreasing step functions of

Table 2-1.   Typical Residential Tariff Schedule

First 100 kwh	3.02¢ per kwh
Next 200 kwh	2.20¢ per kwh
Next 200 kwh	2.00¢ per kwh
Next 500 kwh	1.80¢ per kwh
Additional kwh	1.72¢ per kwh

[f]In view of the obvious economic benefit such sales offer to all consumers (again assuming that incremental cost of production are covered) utility commissions generally favor them. See, for example, *Re Public Service Co. of Oklahoma*, 25 FPC 656, 38 PUR3d 384 (FPC, 1961); *Illinois Coal Operators' Assn. v. Peoples Gas Light & Coke Co.*, 7 PUR(NS) 403 (1934).

[g]See *Re Wisconsin Public Service Corporation*, 7 PUR(NS) 1, 11, 13 (Wisc., 1934); *Re Boston Consolidated Gas Co.*, 14 PUR(NS), 433 (Mass., 1936); and *Croydon Syndicate v. Consolidated Edison Co.*, 59 PUR(NS), 103, 72 N.Y.S. 2d 836 (N.Y. Sup. Ct., 1947).

[h]In *Re Kargman* 99 PUR(NS) 411, 412 (Mass., 1953); *Re Promotional Practices of Electric and Gas Utilities*, 65 PUR3d 405, 515 (Conn., 1966); and *Re Promotional Practices of Electric and Gas Utilities*, 69 PUR3d 317 (Ill., 1967).

[i]See, for example, *In Re Wisconsin Michigan Power Company*, 321 PUR3d, 321, 337 (FPC, 1964); *Otter Rail Power Company*, 33 PUR(NS) 257, 267 (FPC, 1940); *Re Kings County Lighting Company*, 70 PUR(NS) 374, 421-423 (N.Y., 1947); *Re Brooklyn Gas Company*, 70 PUR(NS) 33 (N.Y., 1947). It is arguable that this situation prevails only when the utility is the moving force behind a rate increase filing and not when a proceeding is initiated *sua sponte* by a Commission or at the behest of a third person. See *Bel Oil Corp. v. FPC*, 255 F.2d 548, 554 (CA 5, 1958). However, with the certainty of ever increasing rates this caveat would appear of but historical significance.

quantity consumed. The energy charge is based on the number of kilowatt hours used. This may either be one hundred kilowatts for one hour or one kilowatt for one hundred hours or any other mathematical combination that yields the same measured energy. The separate demand component derives from the fact that electric power cannot be stored (except in batteries, of course). Accordingly, generating facilities are designed to provide sufficient kilowatt capacity to meet peak demands. The demand component is intended to take into account the capacity needed to meet the customer's peak demand. The costs of holding this capacity available but unused are significant, and the two-part energy/demand tariff is an effort, albeit a crude one, to reflect these different cost components.

Consider an illustrative energy/demand tariff as in Table 2-2. (Such a rate schedule is called a Hopkinson demand schedule and was first introduced in 1892.) For any two customers subject to this schedule (assuming equal energy consumption), the consumer with the highest "load factor"[j] will pay the lowest average price. If a customer increases his energy consumption without increasing his maximum kilowatt demand, or increases his average use more than proportionally, his load factor will rise and his average price fall. Conversely, a fall in load factor means an increase in average price.

A Hopkinson demand schedule, then, penalizes erratic loads and rewards even loads. The penalty is for causing capacity to be held available but not used; the reward is for requiring less capacity to be held available for

Table 2-2. Typical Hopkinson Tariff

Energy Charge	
First 1,000 kwh	2.50¢ per kwh
Next 1,000 kwh	2.00¢ per kwh
Next 5,000 kwh	1.60¢ per kwh
Next 10,000 kwh	1.40¢ per kwh
Next 15,000 kwh	1.20¢ per kwh
Next 20,000 kwh	.90¢ per kwh
Next 150,000 kwh	.75¢ per kwh
Additional kwh	.70¢ per kwh
Demand Charge	
First 2 KW	$2.25 per KW
Next 18 KW	$2.00 per KW
Next 80 KW	$1.50 per KW
Additional KW	$1.25 per KW

[j]Load factor is defined as the ratio of the average load during a designated period to the peak or maximum load during the same period. A high ratio means a relatively steady load; a low ratio is a more erratic load.

infrequent use. But does the Hopkinson Demand Tariff actually work to the benefit of the system as a whole? That is, does it minimize or even reduce the amount of excess capacity in the system through an efficient and effective set of incentives?

Clearly, it does not accomplish these beneficial results with certainty and that is the problem. The Hopkinson tariff does encourage each customer to distribute his demands on kilowatt capacity more evenly over the daily cycle. But that does not necessarily benefit the system as a whole. The incentive for each customer to distribute his demands evenly is as likely as not to make matters worse. Cost minimization requires an even distribution of demand on the system as a whole. We are interested in the distribution of individual demands only as they affect the entire system.

In Figure 2-2 the heavy line describes a hypothetical system load over a 24-hour cycle. The lighter line describes the load of a particular customer over the same cycle. Suppose the customer responds to the Hopkinson incentive to even out his demand. He does so by adding a block of demand (shaded area) during the 8 p.m.–4 a.m. period. This improves *his* load factor and results in a lower price per kilowatt. Unfortunately, the additional demand increases the peak demand on the system, which now must maintain more excess capacity than previously.

In Figure 2-3, consider a customer who contemplates shifting a portion of his load from the 8 p.m.–4 a.m. period to the 4 a.m.–noon period. If he does so, the distribution of his load will be less even and his price per kilowatt will increase. Simultaneously, however, the peak demand on the system would decrease. Yet, the Hopkinson tariff penalizes such a shift.

In Figure 2-4, consider the customer who has a 100 percent load factor, a case where a Hopkinson tariff has produced an even pattern of load (the straight line). It is clear that the system, which has peaks caused by other customers, would benefit if the customer shifted the pattern of his load, changing his 100 percent load factor, as indicated by the dotted lines. But the Hopkinson tariff would penalize such a shift.

Finally, there is a limiting case in which the Hopkinson tariff works well—that is, when *all* customers distribute their loads perfectly evenly. Then it must follow that the system load is distributed perfectly evenly. The system load factor is 100 percent and each individual load factor is 100 percent. But that is the limiting case; what is true at the extreme is not necessarily true anywhere else.

If, for example, a system has a 98 percent load factor (very slight unevenness), the system will not necessarily move in the direction of 100 percent load factor by persuading all customers to even their own load. It depends on just how the customers respond. If even a single customer does not achieve a perfect pattern, then the thing to do is to encourage other customers to produce offsetting unevenness in their loads. In short, for a Hopkinson tariff to work with assured effectiveness, it must work flawlessly.

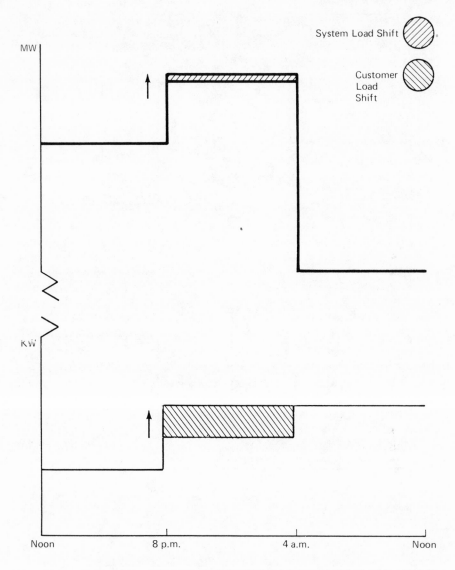

Figure 2-2. System Load and Customer Load Curves

The balance of the price paid for electricity is composed of sundry service charges, fuel cost adjustments, charges for special service, and a variety of discounts, all of which vary widely among utilities. Too, there are other types of rate schedules in use,[k] but the vast bulk of electric power sold at retail in the United States is sold under one of the types of schedule described here, or some variation thereof.

[k]See Garfield and Lovejoy, *Public Utility Economics*, Englewood Cliffs, N.J.: Prentice-Hall, 1964; Russell Caywood, *Electric Utility Rate Economics*, New York: McGraw-Hill, 1956.

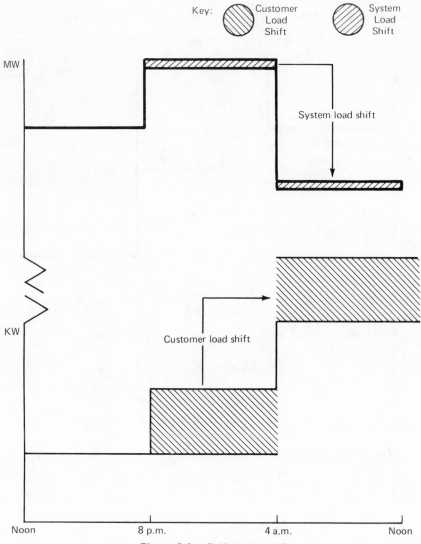

Figure 2-3.   Shifting Load Curves

RATE DESIGN CRITERIA

After utilities design rate schedules, regulators must decide if the various prices are just and reasonable. What is meant by the statutory standard of "just and reasonable"? Just and reasonable prices are those which fall within a zone of

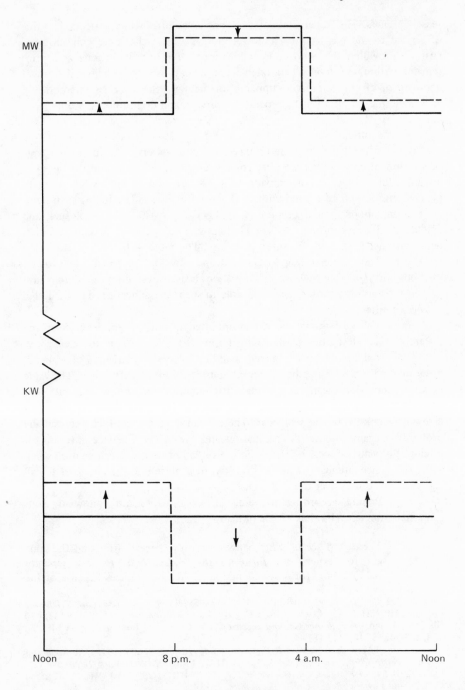

Figure 2-4. Exceptional Load Curves

reasonableness. The upper limit of this zone is the price which reflects the value of service to the customer.[1] The lower limit is a price that covers the utilities' cost of providing the service, including investor return.[m] As long as a price remains within the zone of reasonableness, it may usually be adjusted to meet competition from alternate suppliers of energy. Such prices theoretically encourage the corporation to provide the service, and do not unjustly enrich the consumer at the expense of the producer or vice versa, or one consumer at the expense of another.

The difficulty in determining the cost of service is due to the large proportion of costs which are joint costs, that is, which can not be attributed to an individual, or group of individuals. Costs are conventionally classified as (1) customer costs, associated with serving a given class and including such items as metering, hookup and accounting; (2) energy costs, the cost of fuel; and (3) "demand" or capacity costs, including such items as plant and facilities, depreciations, taxes and return on rate base. The most difficult costs to assign are capacity costs. According to Garfield and Lovejoy (p. 159), some 30-odd methods for allocating these costs have been devised over the years. None have proven satisfactory; consequently the role of such cost allocations in rate design has been limited.

Value of service, as a concept used in rate design, depends on the different price elasticities of demand of the separable markets for electricity, e.g., residential or industrial. Indeed, without different elasticities of demand, value of service would not be a relevant consideration in tariff design. The value of service criterion means simply that different users may be charged different prices for what is essentially the same service. It is the familiar notion of charging what the traffic will bear. There is an apparent conflict between the prohibition against undue discrimination and the value of service criterion for pricing. But value of service pricing did not represent undue discrimination when value of service pricing enabled the utility to achieve a lower unit cost for all classes of customers over the long run.

Pricing according to value of service does not follow rigorous economic principles, but has a logic of its own.

> The *difference in value* between gas for space heating and the same gas for other uses *furnishes the logical basis for the separate classification* for respondents' space-heating services because of the

---

[1]See *Smyth v. Ames*, 1969 U.S. 466, 547 (1898); *Re New York Telephone Co.*, 87 PUR(NS) 1, 15 (Conn., 1951); *City of Chicago v. Sprague*, 9 PUR(NS) 433, 470 (Ill., 1935); and *Iowa-Illinois Gas and Electric Co. v. Commerce Commission*, 34 PUR 3d 228, 233-34, 167 N.E. 2d 414.

[m]*Norfolk & Western R.R. Co. v. Conley*, 236 U.S. 605 (1915); *Re Rochester Gas & Electric Corp.*, 33 PUR(NS) 393, 522 (N.Y., 1940); *Re New York Telephone Co.*, PUR1923B 545; *Re Milwaukee Gas Light Co.*, 51 PUR(NS) 299, 310 (Wis., 1943); and Garfield and Lovejoy, *Public Utility Economics*, p. 138.

fundamental principle of rate making that reasonable utility rates cannot result in charges for any utility service which are more than such service is worth to the customer. This principle was established in *Smyth v. Ames* (1898). . . .[n] (Emphasis added.)

Value of service pricing has also been justified as a means of promoting growth in the industry.

Rates should be designed to hold existing business, *promote new business*, be just and equitable to the customer, promote good public relations and provide a fair return to the utility thereby making it possible to *attract new capital to meet the industry's growth*. No formula can be designed to attain these ends, but two basic factors must be constantly kept in mind—cost of service and value of service.[o] (Emphasis added.)

Even if value of service pricing at one time enabled a utility to take advantage of economies of scale, increasing costs over time have tended to negate the validity of this pricing criterion. In addition, value of service pricing does not reflect the incidence of costs, and may give inappropriate price signals to consumers.

It is apparent that the exercise of judgment or administrative and managerial discretion in rate design has important implications. It permits rate design to involve a broad spectrum of noneconomic considerations. Income redistribution is accomplished and other social goals are pursued. These consequences of rate design may or may not be explicit, and may conflict with that aspect of the public interest a regulatory agency is charged with protecting. It is essential in this current period of environmental concern, energy shortages, and rising prices that objective nondistorted pricing practices are developed. Accordingly, we suggest that the principles of economic efficiency and marginal cost pricing be applied to electric utilities.

We turn now to a discussion of those principles.

ECONOMIC PRINCIPLES FOR PRICING ELECTRICITY

According to Kahn, "The single most widely accepted rule for the governance of the regulated industries is [to] regulate them in such a way as to produce the same results as would be achieved by effective competition, if it were feasible.[p]

---

[n]*Re Milwaukee Gas Light Co., et al.*, 51 PUR(NS) 299, 306, 307 (1943), cited in Garfield and Lovejoy, *op. cit.*, p. 137.

[o]American Gas Association, *Report of Rate Committee*, New York: American Gas Association, 1953, p. 3, cited in Garfield and Lovejoy, *op. cit.* p. 138.

[p]Alfred Kahn, *The Economics of Regulation*, Vol. 1, New York: John Wiley, 1970.

The result that would flow from effective competition is described in economic theory as a "welfare optimum." That means (loosely) that the welfare or well-being of all individuals taken as a group cannot be improved. To an economist the question becomes: Given a distribution of income, how can scarce resources be allocated so that no individual is made better off without making another individual worse off?

If all markets were competitive and functioned perfectly, a welfare optimum would result and all resources would be channeled to their most efficient use. The fundamental rule for achieving this state of efficiency requires that the price of a good or service equal its marginal cost. Outside the theoretical world of perfect competition, some variation in pricing at marginal cost may be accepted, but marginal cost remains the point of departure.

Electric utilities, as presently organized, constitute a so-called "natural monopoly." Regulation was established to prevent them from exercising monopoly power. Marginal cost still remains the principal theoretical criterion for determining appropriate price. A problem that may arise from marginal cost pricing is that revenues to the utility may be much higher or lower than the revenue which the regulatory authority would consider a "fair return." Consequently, a total profit ceiling or revenue constraint is imposed by the regulatory authority. If pricing at marginal cost produced either a deficit or a surplus of revenues, a rule would be required which, while minimizing the departure from marginal cost, achieved the administratively determined profitability target. We defer for the moment the form such a rule might take (see Appendix B) and consider the appropriate measure of marginal cost.

In the simple model of perfect competition, efficiency requires that price equal short-run marginal cost (SMRC). However, there is general agreement among economists who have studied the regulated industries that "the practically achievable benchmark for efficient pricing is more likely to be a type of average long-run incremental cost (LRIC) computed for a large, expected incremental block of sales, instead of SRMC."[q] There are several reasons for this departure from the narrow ideal of the perfectly competitive model. Either explicit or close to the surface in each justification for rejecting SRMC as the sole criterion for rate design are the practical limits and constraints on the regulating authorities.

Several examples clarify this. First, marginal cost pricing may lead to profits greater or less than an administratively determined target. A somewhat facile response from economic theory is either to subsidize the utility or tax

---

[q]Kahn, *op. cit.*, p. 85. See also James C. Bonbright, *Principles of Public Utility Rates*, New York: Columbia University Press, 1961, pp. 331-336; Charles F. Phillip, Jr., *The Economics of Regulation*, Homewood, Ill.: Chas. Irwin, 1969, pp. 320-394; James R. Nelson, ed., *Marginal Cost Pricing in Practice*, Englewood Cliffs, N.J.: Prentice-Hall, 1964, p. 70; and *The Theory of Marginal Cost and Electricity Rates*; Organization for European Economic Cooperation (OEEC), 1958, p. 55.

away excess profits; but in fact, regulators seldom have the authority either to tax or subsidize. The basic operating principle in the regulatory process is that "rates as a whole must equal total costs."

A second difficulty in using SRMC in pricing is the extreme variability of SRMC. For an electric utility, given its unusually high proportion of fixed (capacity) costs, SRMC during off-peak hours is almost entirely fuel cost, and is relatively small. SRMC remain low until the system approaches peak capacity at which point they rise sharply. Such unstable prices are held to be undesirable.

> It would also be highly vexatious to buyers, who would be quick to find discrimination in departures from uniform prices, who would be put to great expense to be informed about prices that were constantly changing, and whose ability to make rational choices and plan intelligently for the future would be seriously impaired (Kahn, p. 84).

Similarly, Bonbright argues that highly variable prices impede rational decision making by electricity consumers since they make their investments in electricity-using devices on the basis of existing rate schedules which they expect to remain in effect for some time. In addition,

> low "incremental cost" rates which, at the time of their establishment, seemed well justified by their compensatory character at a later time (may fail) to cover even their out-of-pocket costs (Bonbright, p. 334).

The expensive and time consuming administrative procedures which attend rate making are well known. Adjustments to tariff schedules for relatively short term variations in cost were not feasible given the absence of suitable metering devices to monitor consumer patterns of demand.

In sum, most economists argue that rates should be based on long-run incremental cost, but that rate schedules may also be designed so as to reflect some short term variation in costs, for example, by the use of interruptible rates or lower rates for service that is characteristically off-peak such as controlled residential water heating.[r]

Finally, the greatest variation in the cost of producing electric power is over the daily load cycle, and it is this cycle which costs should, ideally, follow. However, few customers are presently metered in such a way as to record this daily variation in consumption. Hence, pricing policy must be geared to longer run cost variations.

---

[r]Kahn, *op. cit.*, p. 108.

DECREASING COSTS, PRICE DISCRIMINATION, AND LOAD LEVELING

Several references to decreasing costs have already been made. However, the invocation of some (typically ill-defined) notion of decreasing cost is so prevalent in discussions of utility pricing practices that we deal with the subject again, briefly.

Price discrimination is defined as variation in price not based on variation in cost. Price discrimination may be acceptable in the case where the price that equals marginal cost is such that either an excess or deficit in total revenues results. In the case of the electric power industry, price discrimination may be employed in order to generate additional revenue sufficient to cover total cost or to restrict revenue to the level of the profit constraint.

There are probably few genuine cases of decreasing short-run *marginal* costs in the electric utility industry. Over the relevant range of short-run costs—i.e., over the actual variation in load on a utility system—these costs are likely to be constant for low system loads and rising at higher loads. This is because at minimum load a system operates with its most efficient plants. Incremental costs are basically fuel costs. As load increases, less efficient plants are brought on line. Since the most efficient plants are typically the largest (with some important exceptions in the case of the very large plants), costs increase as the system draws on a series of successively less efficient plants.

Whereas we have just referred to *increasing* costs, the precise same set of circumstances may, with different definitions, provide instances of *decreasing* costs as well. Consider the short-run situation in which capacity does not vary. Four cost concepts are significant: (1) short-run marginal costs, (2) short-run average variable costs, (3) short-run average fixed costs, and (4) short-run average total costs.

Short-run average variable costs are composed of the weighted average per kilowatt hour of variable cost for each plant utilized. These costs are also likely to be rising as service expands in the relevant range, although at a lesser rate. Spreading fixed capital costs, as kwh sales increase in a period in which capacity is not varied, will by definition reduce short-run average fixed costs. This conclusion is a mathematical certainty, whose converse is no less true. Combining both short-run average cost concepts into a short-run average total cost can lead to an increasing, constant or decreasing schedule. But what is the significance for pricing policy of even a short-run average total cost that decreases?

A pricing scheme which incorporates the notion of decreasing average total costs may be defended on the grounds that total economic welfare of the society is enhanced if, during a period of excess capacity, consumers pay their marginal (i.e., variable) cost and make some contribution to fixed costs.

Thus, decreasing short-run average total costs are the basis for much of the promotional activities of the electrical utilities. The objective is load leveling, or reducing excess capacity by promoting off-peak use of power, e.g., for water heating. Those who oppose promotional practices on the grounds of significant external costs are often prepared to concede the efficiency gains of increased off-peak consumption, but would respond that the utilities should consider peak shaving as well as load leveling, hence the "save-a-watt" campaigns of recent years. On grounds of economic efficiency, the opponents of promotional off-peak sales may have conceded too much. Certainly there are efficiency gains from increased off-peak consumption, but are there *net* efficiency gains? There are significant external costs associated with any increase in energy production. The relevant economic question is whether the welfare gains from increased "private efficiency" exceed the increased social costs of that production. Until that calculus is done, the economic rationale for load leveling is severely qualified.

It must be kept in mind that the practical and pragmatic principles for electric rate design emerged from a particular historical context, and that theoretical criteria, too, while more abstract, were also shaped for an existing set of circumstances. For decades, it had been virtually axiomatic that as the industry grew its costs and prices would decline. But as conditions change, so too should our responses and initiatives. We will want to continue to enjoy the benefits of electric power, and we will wish to consume even greater quantities of it. Yet, while we appreciate its value, we must recognize its cost.

In the next chapter, we consider an approach to pricing which recognizes not only the total amount of those costs, but the pattern of their incidence as well. The approach itself is not new: it is already applied to many goods and services, including movie tickets, travel fares, and telephone rates. In principle, it applies to any case where the difference between demand and capacity available to meet that demand varies widely over a temporal cycle; that is, wherever there is a marked difference between peak and off-peak demand. Electric power is an archetypical case.

Chapter Three

Pricing: Its Potential

PEAK LOAD PRICING

Peak load or time differentiated pricing is a type of tariff that varies according to the level of kilowatt demand on a utility system over a daily and seasonal cycle (see also Appendix B). It is based on the theory of marginal cost pricing which postulates that producers should (and in a competitive economy will) expand production so long as consumers are willing to pay the incremental (or marginal) cost of each additional unit of output.

For the electric utilities there are several categories of costs with vastly different characteristics. The price that a consumer should pay for service is the sum of the marginal costs in each category. For example, there are separable costs for the generating plant, the transmission network, and the distribution network, as well as a portion of total costs that does not fit any of these major classifications. Each of these would be accounted for "at the margin" in an ideal price schedule. Since administrative costs also increase with the complexity of the tariffs, a practically achievable variation of marginal cost pricing is our objective.

The reader should note that the argument for peak load pricing is usually phrased in terms of savings in capital expenditures. Unless the elasticity and cross-elasticity of demand for peak power is zero, less capacity is required to meet demand under peak load pricing tariffs than under time uniform tariffs. It is the foregone expenditure in additional capacity which constitutes the bulk of the savings from peak load pricing. An additional source of savings deserves mention, however, in the days of a shortage of fossil fuels.

A power generating system consists of a mix of plants to serve different types of loads, i.e., peak load, intermediate load, and base load. Each of these types has a different ratio of capital costs to energy (fuel) cost. These vary inversely. High capital costs are associated with relatively low energy or operating costs, and vice versa. Since peak loads occur only a few hours per year, it makes sense to meet the peak demand with plants which have relatively low capital costs; energy costs will not be significant in any case. Conversely, base loads require plants which economize on fuel, and relatively higher capital costs are therefore acceptable.

Exactly which mix of plants is appropriate to a particular system will depend on the time distribution of the system load. However, where peak load pricing results in a flattening of the load distribution (without an increase in the total load) fuel savings will result since more demand will be met by more energy efficient base load and intermediate load plants. Peak load plants which squander fuel in the interest of saving on capital investment will be required less often.

The potential savings in capital investment will probably overshadow whatever fuel savings may result from peak load pricing. But the current fuel shortage adds additional impetus for peak load pricing. Additionally, under current tariffs consumers who voluntarily reduce electricity consumption may find that there is a financial penalty for doing so. The consumer's electric bill may be a function only of kwh sales, but costs to the utility are much less so. In most cases the lost revenue exceeds any short-run cost savings, thus leading to pressure for revenue increases as utilities seek "conservation" adjustments. Tying electricity prices more closely to costs as with peak load pricing will reward energy conservation and penalize excesses. It will encourage conservation when the benefits are greatest. Greater consumer acceptance is likely by those consumers who are outraged at the thought of higher prices because they followed conservation appeals.

DERIVING THE APPROPRIATE PRICES[a]

Cost data and other information are kept according to accounting formats useful for present pricing strategies. Since peak load pricing has not been tried in the United States, it is not surprising that there are deficiencies in the data available to a particular utility system. But while refinements in cost and load data collection would be helpful, it is nonetheless possible to demonstrate how existing empirical information may be used to derive a set of time-differentiated prices.

Demand or Capacity Costs

The size of the required generating capacity is determined by the level of maximum or peak demand on the utility system.[b] The first approxi-

---

[a]We are indebted here to Donald N. DeSalvia, whose article "An Application of Peak Load Pricing," *Journal of Business* 45 (1969): 458, we follow closely.

[b]Note that the reference is to *system* peak. There are creatures of utility accounting such as "customer class peak," "customer peak" and others. None of these is relevant here—nor, we would add, particularly useful elsewhere.

mation of capacity cost is the long-run incremental cost of this capacity, plus desired reserve capacity. This estimate of capacity costs, apportioned among all the peak users according to their on-peak demands, will be the basis of the peak charge.

Note, however, that under certain conditions the peak charges may be imposed during certain nonpeak hours. The capacity charge will be set so as to constrain demand to the level of supply at any particular time. Supply, or capacity, is in fact variable. It is not simply the maximum power output of the system at any time during the year.

For example, assume that hydro capacity forms 20 percent of the total capacity of a hypothetical system. Thermal power provides 80 percent. If the hydro capacity is 100 megawatts and the thermal capacity is 400 megawatts, the maximum output of the system during the year is 500 megawatts. Suppose the system peak is in July, but that in July reservoirs are nearly empty, stream flow is minimal, and the hydro capacity is therefore not available. *Available* capacity is limited to 400 megawatts. In order to provide additional capacity, the generating plant would have to be expanded. Consequently, any demands which would require that expansion should be charged a peak rate.

Similar hypothetical cases could be drawn up for generating plants which were not available at the time of system peak due to scheduled maintenance or forced outage. The important point to note is that peak charges are applied to periods which approach or reach *available* capacity and not simply maximum capacity. For this analysis we assume that available capacity at the time of peak and maximum capacity are the same. In pricing, potential peak hours, rather than the actual single hour of maximum peak demand, are most important.

Most electric utilities have a distinct seasonal peak, either winter or summer. In some cases, the maximum winter and summer demands are approximately the same. But by far the greatest variation in demand is over the daily cycle. For purposes of rate design, the peak is defined as those hours in which the system is operating at or close to maximum available plant capacity. Figure 3-1 is an average daily load model for an illustrative electric utility during certain winter months. Figure 3-2 is a similar curve for several summer months. The peak is defined as those hours during the year in which demand exceeds 85 percent of capacity. That occurs in the illustration only during the winter months. Had the summer and winter peaks been less distinct, some summer hours would also have fallen within the defined peak. Thus the peak is defined as the hours between 4:00 p.m. and 8:00 p.m. on weekdays during the months of November through February, which is a total of approximately 340 hours during the year. The number of peak hours may of course vary widely among utility systems. Standard models for peak load pricing allocate capacity costs only to the peak hours. No capacity costs are assigned to off peak consumption, which is instead charged off peak running or variable costs.

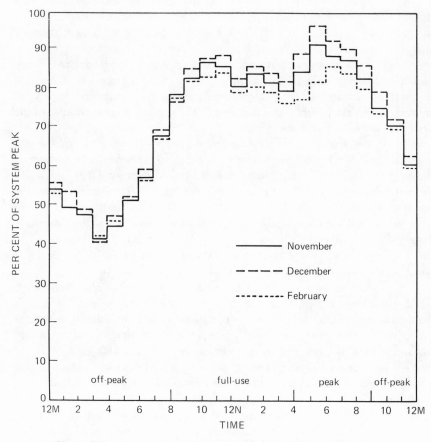

Figure 3-1. Average Load Model for Selected Winter Months

Transmission Costs

Clearly, transmission facilities requirements are related to peak consumption. But determining the charge to be derived from marginal transmission costs is somewhat more troublesome than capacity charges because there are two geographical sources of variation in cost. First, transmission facilities may serve well defined geographical areas, presenting capacity limitations apart from those of the whole system. That is, a system may be operating at less than maximum generating capacity, but the transmission lines to a particular area may be strained to the limit. Second, losses do occur as power is transmitted over greater distances although some lines carry power more efficiently than others. The first source of geographical variation may be ignored in the interest of tariff

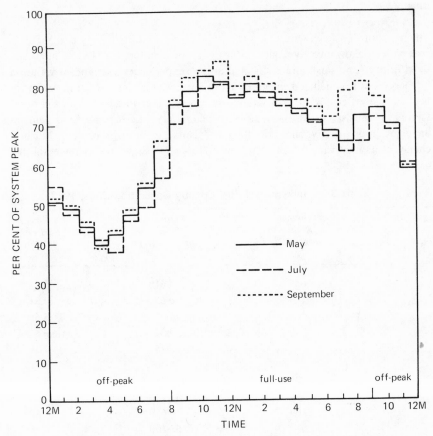

Figure 3-2. Average Load Model for Selected Summer Months

simplification,[c] especially in the larger, integrated grid systems; the better integrated the system the less one is able to attribute cost causally to a particular area.

In practice, data concerning losses in transmission are recorded only in the form of totals for the whole system, which makes it impossible to precisely calculate the marginal transmission cost. This imperfection must therefore be ignored. In short, subject to the above qualifications, transmission costs should be allocated in much the same manner as generation costs—i.e., on a marginal capacity cost basis—although refinement is possible and perhaps desirable.

---

[c]In tariff design, what is possible is not always practical. Tariff complexity imposes its own variety of costs.

Energy Cost

The remaining cost element with a temporal character is the energy cost.[d] This is fuel plus an allowance, typically 15 percent, for maintenance. Even a moderate sized utility (or a small interconnected utility) experiences a significant variation in energy costs as demand increases above the base load level. Energy costs vary because the efficiency of plants varies due to age, location, fuel used, and other factors. The least costly, most efficient plants serve the base load. As demand increases, more costly and less efficient plants are brought on line. Further, energy costs may vary for any given unit. Table 3-1 shows the incremental fuel

Table 3-1. Incremental Fuel Cost by Generating Units, 1973

Unit	Nominal Rating (megawatts)	Output Range (megawatts)	Incremental Fuel Cost (mills/kwh)
1	625	0-610	3.3
2,3,4,5	100	0-65	4.81
		65-97	5.68
6,7	90	0-35	6.57
		35-75	7.55
		75-90	9.51
8	95	0-55	6.29
		55-95	7.62
9	100	0-65	5.80
		65-100	6.85
10,11	100	0-65	4.79
		65-100	5.56
12,13	220	0-110	4.58
		110-210	5.32
14	91	0-35	6.47
		35-88	7.34
15	100	0-40	5.87
		40-75	6.54
		75-92	7.74
16	100	0-65	5.40
		65-94	6.27
17	99	0-65	5.74
		65-94	6.60

[d]As with capacity costs, hydroelectricity is again a special case. The energy costs of hydro are virtually zero, except for pumped storage hydro which involves the use of other energy sources, including fossil fuels, during off peak periods. Pumped storage is of growing significance.

cost for the generating units of a large Eastern U.S. utility over various ranges of individual plant output. Table 3-2 shows this data rearranged to indicate the incremental fuel cost for the whole system.

Table 3-2.   Cumulative Capacity in Order of Incremental Fuel Cost, 1973

Unit	Maximum Output (megawatts)	Cumulative Output (megawatts)	Incremental Fuel Costs (mills/kwh)
1	610	610	3.3
12	110	720	4.58
13	110	830	4.58
10	65	895	4.79
11	65	960	4.79
2	65	1025	4.81
3	65	1090	4.81
4	65	1155	4.81
5	65	1220	4.81
12	100	1320	5.32
13	100	1420	5.32
16	65	1485	5.40
10	35	1520	5.56
11	35	1555	5.56
2	32	1587	5.68
3	32	1619	5.68
4	32	1651	5.68
5	32	1683	5.68
17	65	1748	5.74
9	65	1813	5.80
15	40	1853	5.87
16	29	1882	6.27
8	55	1937	6.29
14	35	1972	6.47
15	35	2007	6.54
6	35	2042	6.57
7	35	2077	6.57
17	29	2106	6.60
9	35	2142	6.85
14	53	2194	7.34
6	40	2234	7.55
7	40	2274	7.55
8	40	2314	7.62
15	17	2331	7.74
6	15	2346	9.51
7	15	2361	9.51

Here it may be useful to further divide the nonpeak hours of the year into two or more classes. The number of classes is arbitrary, depending on the design of metering equipment and the desire for easily administered tariffs. Some meters, such as those with time switches, will present a limitation on the number of periods. Others, such as remote control frequency sensitive meters, would allow a much greater number of designated periods and therefore prices. The latter are not necessarily more costly than the former.

Returning to Figures 3-1 and 3-2, two nonpeak periods have been designated. "Off peak" is a fairly continuous load which is required throughout the year; "full use" is any level of demand less than peak and greater than, say, 55 percent of maximum demand or whatever the base load is. The remainder is on peak. Energy charges for these periods could be determined from data such as that contained in Table 3-2.

Other Costs

The remaining portion of total costs includes the cost of the distribution network (see Figure 3-3) and general administration costs. Figure 3-3 does not include recurring expenses for billing and administration associated with the distribution networks. The appropriate treatment of distribution costs under marginal cost principles is a charge equivalent to a monthly payment on an interest bearing loan equal to the cost of the distribution facilities required by each consumer to be hooked up to the system. The balance of costs, such as administration, are relatively insignificant and are probably best levied on a per customer basis.

Data are not now kept in a manner which makes the appropriate assignment of distribution costs possible. Although some effort is made to segregate such costs by category of customer, the failure to distinguish between the distribution costs attributable to various customers constitutes cross-subsidization of unknown magnitude. Since by virtue of density of population, in-city residents require fewer feet of cable and poles per customer and therefore are responsible for lower costs than the more dispersed suburban and rural customers, this amounts to a subsidy of an undetermined amount by city dwellers to out-of-city customers. The quantitative importance of such cost differences is highly variable, but may be one of several factors, including analogous water, sewage, and street and highway subsidies, which contribute to such problems as urban sprawl. There may be other, higher costs associated with distribution to urban dwellers such as the need to reinforce existing lines as use per customer increases for hard to reach lines. Variance across the nation is great, but it is a reasonable presumption that the present treatment of distribution costs in some metropolitan areas amounts to a subsidy which few would favor if it were explicitly recognized.

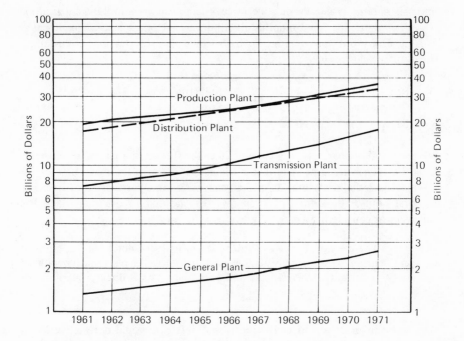

Source: Federal Power Commission, *Statistics of Privately Owned Electric Utilities in the United States*, 1971, p. XLIII.

Figure 3-3. Electric Plant In Service By Function (Classes A and B, Privately Owned Electric Utilities)

TARIFFS UNDER PEAK LOAD PRICING

The prices that would be derived according to the above peak load pricing methodology are interesting—and at first glance startling. DeSalvia (see footnote a) derived the following prices, exclusive of distribution and general administration costs.

Production and Transmission Costs
(based on existing load patterns)

Daily Period	Winter (¢/kwh)	Summer (¢/kwh)
Peak	11.11	—
Full use	0.46	0.46
Off peak	0.30	0.36

Since his data are a decade old, the prices themselves are useful largely as ratios to one another. The fixed monthly distribution and other costs were allocated on an arbitrary but not unreasonable basis to the various categories of customer. The resultant charges were:

Residential	$ 4.84	Industrial	$165.91
Commercial	10.03	Street	
Farm	16.22	lighting	404.67

The peak period charge is twenty-four times the full use charge and thirty-seven times the off peak charge. The factor which accounts for the magnitude of the differentials is the brief duration of the peak—348 hours per year or 4 percent of the total hours.[e] In addition, low energy costs are due in part to the fact that DeSalvia was considering a mixed hydro-fossil fuel system.

> The average demand could be serviced with a much smaller physical plant. Thus, a considerable portion of the firm's capacity with its concomitant investment and operating costs is directly attributable to peak consumption.[f]

In practice, price differentials of this size would not be warranted since a drastic change in consumption patterns would result, and should be anticipated in the first promulgated set of time-differentiated prices. All customers would seek means of avoiding peak kilowatt hour consumption. Most of the reduction in consumption would surely be shifted to nonpeak periods. Some would result from more efficient use of that power which necessarily is consumed on peak, and some uses would be dispensed with altogether. Since there is no relevant prior experience with time-differentiated rates in the U.S. the net result of the shifts and reductions can only be guessed at. As experience and data are accumulated, the elasticities and cross-elasticities of peak and off peak demand could be estimated and used in further efforts to reduce excess investment and resource misallocation.

By making some conservative and not unreasonable assumptions about shifting demand patterns, one can derive a set of prices that are more likely to be appropriate after peak load pricing has been in effect. DeSalvia assumed a 5 percent decrease in the winter peak, which reduced it to the level of the "full use" period. He further assumed a 5 percent increase in summer full use consumption, which raised that to the level of winter full use. DeSalvia then assigned a proportion of the capacity costs to some of the 3,408 full use hours.

---

[e]For comparison, under the French "Green Tariff," of the winter hours 12.5 percent are peak, 20.8 percent intermediate, and 66.7 percent off peak. Of the summer hours, none are designated peak, 33.3 percent are intermediate, and 66.7 percent are off peak.

[f]DeSalvia, *op. cit.*, p. 469.

The capacity cost having been spread over so many more hours, the differentials decreased considerably. The following prices resulted.

Production and Transmission Charges
(based on a changed load pattern)

Period	Winter (¢/kwh)	Summer (¢/kwh)
Peak	2.04	–
Full use	1.60	1.45
Off peak	0.30	0.30

These differentials are more realistic; they reveal the extremely high cost (as reflected in cost determined prices) of sharp daily peaks and excess capacity most of the day and year.[g] And they suggest that even much flattened load curves will support significant price differentials.

It is important to note that these prices would apply to all customers. The sole determinants of the amount of the electric bill are the total consumption, the time of consumption, and the cost of patching into the system. Eliminated are such spurious considerations as what the power is used for (residential, industrial, or other uses) and the quantity consumed during the month. Should social or political reasons dictate that some customers are to be provided electricity at subsidized rates (religious and rural customers sometimes obtain service at explicitly preferential rates) that subsidy may be applied easily; but inadvertent subsidies such as those provided by present rates would be abolished. DeSalvia postulated that had his prices been in effect for the time at which he made his calculations, slightly more revenue would have been generated than under the conventional rates.

Let us compare the incentives implicit in present nontime differentiated rates with those of peak load pricing. The load curves shown in Figures 3-1 and 3-2 result from uniform prices over time. Nontime differentiated rate schedules do not, by definition, affect the temporal pattern of consumption. Since rates typically decrease as consumption increases, whether kilowatt or kilowatt hour consumption, the incentive is to expand individual consumption. At one time expanded consumption may have tended to occur in off peak hours, but consumption expansion now is as likely as not to be on peak. Existing rate structures continue to provide an incentive via lower prices to a customer who exacerbates capacity requirements even though the costs of new capacity are higher than costs associated with existing capacity.

Time-uniform rates carry a portion of capacity costs in all hours,

---

[g]The approximate 7 to 1 price differential between on and off peak derived by DeSalvia compare to about 4 to 1 price differentials under the Green Tariff. See R. Meek, "An Application of Marginal Cost Pricing: The 'Green Tariff' in Theory and Practice," *Journal of Industrial Economics*, July 1973 and November 1963.

which means there is, in effect, a penalty associated with off peak consumption, because in fact there are no appreciable capacity costs off peak. The size of the penalty is usually a several hundred percent surcharge over actual costs, and off peak consumption is discouraged—albeit to no discernible benefit to producer or consumer.

Peak load pricing, on the other hand, carries a completely opposite set of incentives. It discourages on peak consumption, by charging higher on peak prices and encourages greater use of excess capacity by charging lower prices off peak.

In conclusion, while some of the above may seem overly complex, Turvey[h] has reduced peak load pricing rules to a rather simple form:

> In each period, price is whichever is the greater of:
>
> (a) the running [operating] cost of that capacity which is partly utilized, or
>
> (b) the level required to restrict demand to capacity.

OBJECTIONS OVERRULED

While peak load pricing has not been implemented in the United States,[i] utility managers have considered problems that might occur if it was. In the following passages we consider those mentioned most frequently.

The Shifting Peak

As peak load prices are implemented, changes in the load pattern are to be expected. Conceivable changes are illustrated in Figures 3-4 and 3-5, where consumers have switched demand so as to avoid the peak charge. The result has been to reduce consumption during the period defined in the price schedule as "peak," and increase the demand during non peak periods. Figure 3-4 presents the more probable case. Neither, however, represents a problem. The solution is to redefine the peak and issue revised tariffs. Turvey points out that since consumer reactions are slow, "peak-shifting does not in practice present an intractable problem."[j]

---

[h]R. Turvey, *Economic Analysis and Public Enterprises*, Totowa, N.J.: Rowman and Littlefield, 1971, p. 74.

[i]Peak-off-peak price differentials have been implemented for such use as water and space heating. This is not a true application of marginal cost pricing principles since it is one-sided, i.e., there is an off peak discount but no corresponding on peak premium. Another variation on this theme is "interruptible" rates whereby large consumers receive discounted rates for accepting the possibility that their service may be discontinued on short notice during periods which strain utility capacity. Such "marginalist" pricing schemes in effect here and abroad are discussed in W.G. Shepherd, "Marginal Cost Pricing in American Utilities," *Southern Economic Journal*, 33 (1967): 58.

[j]R. Turvey, *Optimal Pricing and Investment in Electricity Supply*, Cambridge, Mass.: The MIT Press, 1968.

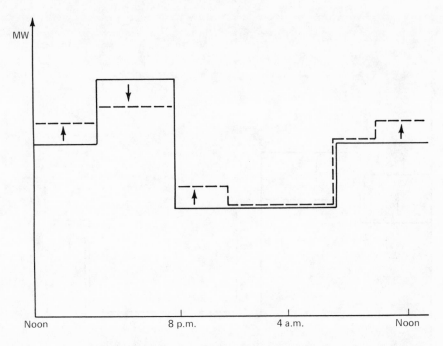

Figure 3-4. System Load Shifting with the Same Peak Period

In any case, note that there could be a considerable difference between the process presently required to design rates, and the procedure which could be used if peak load pricing existed. The typical rate case involves determining the appropriate rate of return on investment, the revenue required to meet that target, and the particular rates which will produce that revenue. A host of horrendously tedious subsidiary questions arise and virtually every point is the subject of exhaustive and disputed testimony. The hearings may take weeks, months or years. But present rate hearings are complicated because almost every issue raised is decided by administrative judgment rather than objective criteria. Peak load pricing would both simplify and significantly reduce the need for rate filings.

1. Peak prices would eliminate the existing incentive to consumers to expand demands on peak, and thus reduce the need for capacity additions. Consequently, utilities would not need to petition as often for rate increases to attract investment capital.

2. Costs are rising over time and significant demand growth is in the tail blocks of declining block rates which are not compensatory. When the need for additional capacity is caused by larger customers as compared to new

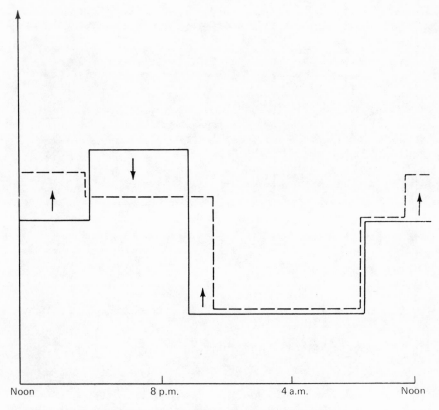

Figure 3-5. Varying Peak Period Load Shifting

customers, this contribution to peak demand costs the utility more than the expansion generates in revenue. Peak load prices, on the other hand, are compensatory at every level of demand. Thus the need for rate hearings diminishes further.

3. Disputes between rate payers as to which class shall bear what portion of the additional revenue requirement are eliminated. The same rates apply to all, and these are determined by objective load criteria. Whether a kilowatt-hour is used to heat a house, light an office building or power a drill press is irrelevant to the price charged. It is no longer necessary to distinguish among customers on any basis except the cost of providing them electricity.

Thus, when peaks shift, it would only be necessary to recompute the tariff schedule according to what can be made into a standardized formula. It will not be necessary to engage the whole range of questions that occupy presently styled hearings. These issues will occasionally be faced, but considerably less often. Any problems associated with peak shifting adjustments will be small by comparison to current rate hearings.

Repair and Maintenance

It is alleged that repair and maintenance schedules may be disrupted by peak load pricing. The argument: while attempts are now made to concentrate repair and maintenance during periods when capacity is idle, under peak load pricing there will be less idle capacity at any one time. Consequently, there will be less opportunity for scheduled outage. The argument implies that higher system load factors are not desirable. It is a curious argument when made on behalf of an industry which has employed selective load building advertising, special night rates, Hopkinson rates, Wright rates, Doherty rates, and moral suasion, all in an effort to achieve higher load factors. Recall that peak period pricing requires prices that are highest when demand approaches available plant capacity. If some portion of plant must be taken out of service for repair or maintenance the period of outage may be defined as peak, although demand at that time does not actually require all the system's installed capacity. It should be recognized that unscheduled outage will occur regardless of pricing strategies, but with a smaller installed capacity required, system reserve requirements will be less under peak load pricing.

Allocation of All Capacity Costs
to Peak Period Demand

The argument has been made that it is neither appropriate nor equitable to assign all the capacity costs to the peak period. Generating plants are specifically designed to serve either base load, intermediate load, or peak load. The plants have different capital and running costs depending on the type of load they are intended to serve. The cost of base load plants might then be assigned to all periods. Costs of intermediate load plants might be assigned to full use and peak periods, and peaking plant costs to the peak period. Such a cost distribution would reflect the respective contribution of each plant to meeting the distributed load. The argument has a deceptive appeal. It may be answered with reference to the concept of opportunity cost.

Economists postulate that the most accurate way to gauge the cost of anything is to consider what is given up when a resource is used for one purpose which precludes its use for other purposes. For example, if a parcel of land may be used to grow either wheat or corn, then the opportunity cost of growing wheat on the land is the value of the corn which cannot be grown, and vice versa. In general, opportunity cost of a resource is the value of the resource in its highest (most valuable) alternative use. The opportunity cost of a scenic gorge may be the value of the hydroelectric power which would be produced if a dam were built.

What is the opportunity cost of using generating capacity that would otherwise be standing idle? To what alternative use can it be put? Obviously, none. The appropriate charge then is zero. If a charge greater than zero is levied on off peak consumption as the objection here proposes, such a penalty would result in under use. Given that a ceiling is imposed on the revenues of the utility, imposing a charge for using nonpeak capacity would require that less than the opportunity cost be charged for peak consumption. The effect is subsidization of peak consumption.

Is it "fair" to assign all capacity costs to the peak period? If the popular will is to have nonpeak users pay the way for on peak users, nothing in logic or economic theory can refute that. But an observation is in order. Sooner rather than later, under the present pricing system the cost to all users, peak and nonpeak alike, will be higher than it otherwise would be. Accordingly, fairness viewed in two time periods may lead to a different conclusion than a static notion of fairness.

Finally, it must be noted that systems are frequently designed and generating capacity installed to meet a peak demand with a dual purpose in mind. A new nuclear or fossil fuel-fired plant may be added to the system in order to reduce the operating costs of off peak service as well as to meet the peak demands when perhaps a lower capital cost but higher operating cost gas turbine plant would have adequately served the peak needs. In such cases, costs are interdependent between on and off peak times. It is appropriate for off peak users to pay some of the additional capacity costs involved since they benefit from this managerial decision.

However, since the operating costs of peak plants are also less under this decision, such savings to peak users must be credited against the off peak price as well. In practice such subtleties may be important as experience with the on and off peak pricing system spreads. At the outset of such a system it is more likely that far rougher estimates of relative cost differences, along the five to one orders reported above, would be followed.[k]

Stability of Rates

Much is properly made of the desirability of achieving stable electricity prices. The charge considered here is that time-differentiated prices are unstable and impede rational planning and decision making by consumers. But in fact, peak load pricing is likely to be more stable than existing rate designs. Peak load prices are not themselves unstable in any meaningful sense. They do vary by time of day; but the pattern of variation is constant. Time-uniform rates, on the other hand, provide incentives which lead to capacity

---

[k]For a further discussion of such subtleties, see: R. Turvey, *Economic Analysis and Public Enterprises, op. cit.*. Turvey refers to such pricing as "mutatis mutandis marginal cost" pricing and contrasts it with "ceteris paribus marginal cost pricing". He attributes these terms to S. Littlechild, "Marginal Cost Pricing with Joint Costs," *The Economic Journal* LXXX (June 1970).

expansion and the need for additional revenues, which is an inherently unstable process. Therefore, concern for stability of electric rates is an argument in favor of peak load pricing.

Metering

Here is the crux of the matter. Peak load pricing should be implemented if and only if, and on such a scale, that the benefits of less excess capacity and improved fuel economy outweigh the cost of the more sophisticated metering that will be required. (An additional potential exists for reduced meter reading and customer billing costs in integrated computerized processes.) Rudimentary and somewhat expensive equipment has been available for some time. To the limited extent to which peak load pricing has been implemented, the chosen equipment has typically employed watt hour meters together with a two- or three-stage time switch. More sophisticated devices are in use which use radio controls to switch modes on a meter or to switch from one meter to another. So-called "ripple control" devices transmit messages to points of consumption via the power line itself. Until recently, however, the requisite metering equipment has been either expensive or beset with technical difficulties, either of which limits application on a wide scale.

Recent technical developments however, have brought the cost of the necessary equipment clearly within the range where it becomes economically feasible to institute time-differentiated pricing. Further, anticipated expenditures for new capacity are of such a magnitude for U.S. electric utilities that even the modest gains from, say, a 5 percent reduction in "requirements" would free those funds for investment in a metering network many times more costly than the existing equipment.[1]

Finally, Vickery[m] has observed that seeking to avoid the cost of metering was

> somewhat as though the operator of a supermarket, chafing at the costs involved in the check-out process, decided to save on these costs by simply weighing each customer's market basket on a scale and charging a uniform price per pound. In a competitive environment such a supermarket would soon be selling only steak and gourmet items while customers went elsewhere for flour, potatoes, and soft drinks. To break even the flat price per pound would have to be pushed up until eventually the store would probably go out of business entirely.

[1]Note this 5 percent deduction in capacity requirements corresponds to the French experience with a more limited form of peak load pricing than is anticipated if the system is adopted in the United States. For a further discussion, see: M. Borteux, "The 'Tarif Vert' of Electricité de France," in *Marginal Cost Pricing in Practice*, James Nelson, ed., Englewood Cliffs, N.J.: Prentice-Hall, 1964.

[m]William Vickery; Testimony before The New York Public Service Commission, Case No. 26402, Albany, N.Y., 1973.

Nor does the metering expense need to be incurred all at once. Some commercial, and industrial customers are already equipped with recording demand meters which may readily be adapted for peak load pricing. Other large consumers could have such equipment installed at a fraction of even one month's electric bill. The optimal procedure would be to start peak load pricing where the costs are lowest and the expected benefits greatest. Equipping progressively smaller consumers may proceed as experience, technology, and expected net benefits justify.

INTERIM PROPOSALS FOR IMPROVING ELECTRICITY PRICING

It is appropriate at this point to reinforce the conclusions reached above concerning the matter of selecting the appropriate price structure. Current pricing practices were developed during a period of increasing returns to scale (in the static narrow economic sense in which larger plants had lower unit costs than smaller ones) and decreasing intertemporal costs, as technological change reduced incremental capacity costs over time. Declining block rate pricing, discussed earlier, may be consistent with economies of scale to the extent they still exist. However, in a period of rising costs over time they no longer make sense.

Peak load pricing discourages the expansion of generating facilities and therefore reduces the need for new higher unit costs of installed capacity. Additionally, low off peak prices based upon energy costs alone would encourage system load leveling and therefore reduce short run operating costs even if energy supply is held constant. Both results are desirable.

Current declining block rate pricing fails with respect to the first, longer run, capacity cost avoidance goal; but in *some* circumstances it may lead to system load leveling and therefore to a reduction in running costs and to a greater spreading of fixed costs. The latter may help reduce the need for price increases, so long as increased use does not lead to system expansion and higher costs. In order for declining block pricing to be beneficial, it is necessary that when a customer increases energy use it will improve the system load factor. This need not be the case, however. Two-part tariffs were designed to lead to this result, but as indicated above the opposite may happen. Therefore, unambiguous statements concerning any benefits of declining block two-part tariff pricing cannot be made. However, the statements made with respect to the beneficial aspects of peak load pricing on both goals can not logically be denied.

To many regulators, utilities, and intervenors peak load pricing may seem too distant a policy even if the distance is as short as two to three years. We believe such a period is possible if decisions are made to go ahead by a utility today. The pressure to make decisions to deal with current and immediate cases is great. Accordingly, we will address some interim measures that can be taken to reform in a partial way the current pricing practicies of the electric utilities. We must note that we do not view such interim steps either as a necessary step prior to peak load pricing or more importantly as a substitute for it. In brief we think the interim steps we shall propose will remedy some of the problems associated with current industry pricing practices, particularly those related to system capacity growth.

We begin with a consideration of the importance of long-run incremental costs (LRIC). LRIC is estimated for additions to system capacity over a reasonable planning horizon.[n] The elements of these costs are

1. Administrative and other overhead costs, including distribution.
2. Capacity costs, where the mix of plants is optimal for the expected load pattern.
3. Energy and related costs.

A charge per kilowatt hour may be derived from these cost estimates. It may be possible to estimate variations in LRIC for a few categories of customers, and it is then probably desirable to do so. This implies that the variation in cost between customer categories is greater than the variation within categories. The proposition may be verified by sampling and analysis. Energy costs so derived may be either a flat per kilowatt hour charge for any customer at any time; or a set of prices, one for each customer category. In the latter case, rate differentials are justified only on the basis of known variations in the cost of serving the different categories.

Different prices charged to different customer classes may be the result of any number of variations in costs to serve. Typically, the most difficult cost to allocate is the demand or capacity costs. While energy costs are fairly readily assigned to particular classes, the total system generating capacity serves all customers, and not necessarily in proportion to the energy consumption of particular classes. That is, the residential class may be responsible for 1/3 of the kilowatt hours consumed, but may require a much greater or lesser proportion of the kilowatt capacity. Suppose, for example, that there is a generating capacity of a certain size, the cost of which is $100 million. What proportion of the $100 million should be collected from each class?

There are thirty-odd methods of making such cost allocations. The method which has most appeal to common sense is to assign the capacity costs in proportion to the capacity used by the respective classes at the time of the system peak. This last qualification is important, for the system peak determines how large a generating system must be (and therefore the total amount of capacity costs), and it does not matter what the extent of the use is at other times since it is always excess capacity—except on peak. This cost allocation is referred to as the "coincidental peak method."

[n]Turvey, *Electricity Pricing, op. cit.*, discusses the computation of long run incremental cost in detail.

The difficulty with the coincidental peak method is that it requires data on how much power is consumed by a particular customer (or class) during the peak period. That information is seldom available, even from sample data. Alternative cost allocation methods also suffer from a paucity of data.

Probably the most frequently employed capacity cost allocation methods are noncoincidental peak[o] and "average and excess demand". Standard texts on utility rate design or "rate economics" describe these methods in detail. Neither has any apparent superiority over the coincidental peak allocation.

After capacity and energy costs have been estimated, it remains necessary to compute a charge to recover those elements of cost which vary by customer and are not associated with either the level of kilowatt capacity required or kilowatt hour consumption. This charge should reflect the costs of the distribution network and administrative costs, and should be levied in the form of a fixed charge per customer.

When the data is available (though it seldom is), geographical variations in cost should be accounted for. Generally, it is possible to estimate distribution costs associated with serving various classes of customer, and the charge then would be equal to the average cost in each class. In effect, each customer pays rent on the distribution facilities he (or his class) uses, plus other customer related costs.

A frequently encountered objection to fixed periodic charges is that consumers do not understand why they should pay something even when they consume no electricity. For this reason, commissions and utilities are inclined to spread the distribution cost over the kilowatt hour charges, typically by creating one or more steps in the kilowatt hour charge, thereby collecting these costs not as a lump sum, but as a surcharge on the first hours of consumption. A small minimum charge is sometimes regarded as feasible.

That consumers are unsettled by a fixed charge does not seem sufficient basis to distort the pricing mechanism. Car owners for example, appear to understand that there are high fixed costs "up front," as it were, associated with owning and operating an automobile. It is likely that most consumers would comprehend the analogy. Further, vacationers expect to pay the phone company a monthly service charge even if they do not make use of their phone.

If it is simply not feasible to have a lump sum charge, pragmatic principles urge that the fixed costs be recouped as early as possible in the energy charge so as to minimize distortion in pricing and the consequent effects on marginal decisions.

---

[o]"This method apportions these costs in proportion to the maximum demands of the different classes and of different individual consumers of service *even though some of these demands, so far from coinciding with the peak load of the company, may be completely off the system peak.* This type of cost apportionment, whatever merit may be claimed for it as a basis of rate making on grounds of "fairness" or on grounds of presumptive value-of-service considerations, *is not really a cost analysis at all and should not be allowed to masquerade as such.*" (Emphasis added.) Bonbright, *op. cit.*, p. 352.

Finally, an estimate ought to be made of the revenues that would be achieved through the tariffs as designed above. Should that level of revenues be greater or lesser than the revenue level required to meet the separately determined allowed rate of return on investment, the tariffs may be marked up or down, as appropriate, from estimated incremental cost. If customer classes have been designated, the greatest percentage markup[p] over cost is in the more inelastic categories. The effect of the change in price on revenues needs to be estimated simultaneously. In the event that available cost data had heretofore suggested no consumer class differentiation, this is a reasonable stage at which to make such distinctions.

The prices suggested by these interim steps are on a kilowatt hour basis, even if separate capacity and energy costs may be identified. This need not be the only alternative. Indeed, a separate two-part (but still flat) energy and capacity charge differentiated by cost of service to customer categories might also be selected to reform existing pricing practices.

A second alternative in the design of rates within a revenue constraint is to keep prices to the level of incremental cost *at the margin*, and to adjust the inframarginal price. In a period of rising (falling) costs, the prices based upon LRIC may produce too much (little) revenue, and initial block prices may be lowered (increased) to keep revenue in line with regulatory constraints and marginal prices in line with costs. If revenue excesses would result by pricing at LRIC, this pricing policy would lead to rising unit tariffs as use increases. Since this is in contrast with current declining block pricing, such proposals are called "rate inversions" or "inverted rate block pricing."

The difficulty with block pricing lies in the information required to set the appropriate marginal price. There are nearly as many margins as there are customers. Consequently, a very careful analysis of consumption patterns is required in order to determine "the margin". In hearings before the Senate Interior Committee, it was suggested that price be set to equal marginal cost for kilowatt hours in excess of 2,000 per year, and to raise (or, more likely, lower) the price below 2,000 kwh as necessary. This might result in extremely low (perhaps zero) prices for that first block. In any case, no *a priori* effort to determine the relevant margin can be made without careful study of a particular utility system, and information requirements alone make it inferior to even the interim steps proposed above.

To Summarize

A procedure to improve rate design until peak load pricing is implemented would

1. Estimate long-run incremental cost.

---

[p]A markup applies to a revenue deficiency. The reader may substitute "markdown" for the case of a surplus of revenues.

2. Convert LRIC to a kilowatt hour charge.
3. Estimate distribution and related costs for each category of customers, and geographical area if possible.
4. Adjust rates in inverse proportion to estimated elasticity of demand to meet revenue objectives.

This procedure, while far from ideal, is cost justified and analytical in approach.

If long-run incremental cost pricing produces revenues in line with historic costs, there is no justification for block rates or variation from LRIC. If costs are increasing, LRIC is a ceiling on rates. Adjustments may be made either by charging different users different prices or by lowering prices for the first quantities in a block rate. It should be noted that it is incorrect to maintain decreasing block rates in the face of increasing LRIC.

INFLATION

Of course, nothing in either existing rate structures or those of the sort proposed take into account the effects of inflation on electric utilities. Inflation hits them particularly hard. Nonregulated firms can generally maintain their relative position in the industrial order by raising prices to keep pace with inflation. Regulated firms must go through costly and time consuming administrative proceedings to do that. Since it is poor public policy to anticipate and thus feed inflation, the utilities are continuously "catching up." The higher the rate of inflation, the more frequent (and bitterly contested) the rate proceedings and the more precarious the fiscal integrity of the utility.

A model for dealing with inflation exists in the so-called fuel adjustment clauses, which permit some utilities to pass on to consumers some or all of the higher (or lower) costs of fuel. This may tend to sap somewhat the competitive vigor of utilities in dealing with fuel suppliers, but the idea is becoming widely accepted as an alternative to increasing the number of rate proceedings. We cautiously propose a similar automatic inflation adjustment clause. It would work as follows:

Each year, a commission would gauge the effect of inflation over the past year on the companies within its jurisdiction. A rate increase would be allowed according to a predetermined, objective index—for example, some fraction or multiple of a standard price index such as the wholesale or consumer price index. It is not important that the chosen index may be flawed; but it is important that the chosen index of rate adjustment not be arbitrarily switched or varied by the commission, as that may lead to court contests each year. The rate increase thus granted would be provisional; that is, subject to a later showing that it was warranted.

About once every four years, the utilities would be required to appear before the commission for ex post review of the revised tariffs. The procedure at that time would be as exhaustive as hearings are at present, with the accounts of the company fully available to the commission and the public for examination. The revenues generated by the inflation adjustment would be imputed to future revenues unless it was demonstrated that they were warranted in the first place.

The disadvantages of this proposal are obvious, but it is better to compare the proposal with the existing situation. The frequency of hearings is significantly diminished, to the benefit both of the company and the commission, which is left free to deal in greater depth with each case. The utilities are better off than before and only somewhat worse off than nonregulated companies; a year lag still exists but some regulatory lags are unavoidable. The bulk of the effect of inflation is accounted for, without being anticipated, and the discriminatory effect of inflation is partially avoided.

A SUMMARY ARGUMENT

Historically, electricity has been priced in such a way as to encourage greater consumption over time and to encourage consumption during off-peak periods. Various pricing strategies, at least at the time they evolved, encouraged consumers to spread their demands more evenly over the load cycle. However, during a period of rising costs over time, it is inappropriate to encourage consumption which requires the addition of new facilities. Consumption in the tail block of declining block rates is typically more likely than not to contribute to peak demand, in which case quantity discounts are perverse.

Peak load pricing meets the dual objectives of discouraging additional power supply investment "requirements," and directly effects system load factor by establishing a direct link between prices and costs. No probabilistic assumptions are required as to the relationship between total quantity consumed and proportionate consumption off-peak.

Other alternatives to current pricing practices are flat or so-called inverted block rates. The latter is expressly designed to limit demand for electric power and would probably do so in an indiscriminate and deleterious fashion. Even in the simplest version of inverted rates, where there are but two blocks, informational requirements as to where to separate the blocks are substantial. Flat rates, on the other hand, would tend less to encourage expansion of electric supply capacity than present rates, but would be similarly indiscriminate between peak and off-peak demands. We believe flat rates to be generally preferable to "inverted rates", but neither should be regarded as any more than an interim reform of declining block rates until such time as peak load pricing could be implemented.

Historically, the regulatory framework within which electricity pricing is determined is most important. It is to that subject that we now turn.

Chapter Four

The Regulatory Framework

INTRODUCTION

There is a gap between what federal and state agencies are authorized to do and what they are doing to regulate the electric power industry. We will review the legal authority, the present practices, and the potential activities of the Federal Power Commission, the Atomic Energy Commission, and the Securities and Exchange Commission to emphasize possibilities for improvements within the existing legal framework. We suggest state activities where that level of government dominates the regulatory procedures. Other federal agencies involved in the electric power industry are briefly described in Appendix C.

Regulation has been passive. The decision of whether and how to expand plants, and the design of rate schedules have been left to the initiative of the utilities. When these initiatives are finally unveiled for regulatory review the attrition of earnings or capacity deficiency has reached the point where even the best intentioned regulator must grant precipitous approval. For this reason we examine the potential for a more active role for the regulator, and suggest new incentives to encourage desired industry performance.

FEDERAL POWER COMMISSION AND STATE REGULATORY AGENCIES

Licensing and Investigations

Federal regulatory supervision over the electric power industry began with the passage, in 1920, of the Federal Water Power Act.[a] A commission made up of the Secretaries of War, Agriculture, and Interior was authorized to license facilities for the production and transmission of electricity which made use of waterways subject to federal jurisdiction—that is, hydro-

---

[a] 41 Stat. 1063, 16 USC 791-823.

electric projects. In 1930 the Federal Power Commission was reconstituted into a five member body appointed by the President with the advice and consent of the Senate.

The Courts have construed the Commission's licensing jurisdiction to cover the licensing of pumped storage projects to be constructed on nonnavigable tributaries of navigable streams where the power ultimately generated could affect interstate commerce.[b] Recently, however, a Federal Appeals Court rejected the argument that a Federal Power Commission license is required as a condition to the construction of steam electric plants that utilize cooling water from navigable streams, but left open the question of whether an FPC license is required where a project is to make use of surplus water from a government dam.[c]

In licensing a hydroelectric project, the Commission is to be concerned with all aspects of the development of the waterway "for other beneficial public uses, including recreational purposes." The Commission must consider the issues of power supply, resource conservation, and environmental protection.[d] Once the Commission has determined that there is a need for the project it must consider all alternatives to accomplish the same objective including reliance upon facilities beyond FPC jurisdiction.[e] The National Environmental Policy Act reinforced the Commission's obligation to undertake its own environmental assessment of the applicant's proposal and, for comparative purposes, of all viable alternatives.[f]

The Commission's conditioning authority is most pervasive at the time of license issuance and has been exercised to offer municipal power agencies the opportunity to purchase excess power from a pumped storage project constructed by investor owned utilities, and to require a private licensee to acquire and maintain public recreational facilities.

Licenses can be issued for periods not to exceed 50 years after which the project can be relicensed to the original licensee, to another utility, to a public authority for nonpower purposes (including domestic water supply) or recaptured (that is, the site taken over) by the United States. In the event of recapture, or relicensing to a new party, the original licensee is to be paid its

---

[b]*FPC v. Union Electric Company*, 381 U.S. 90.

[c]*Chemehuevi Tribe of Indians v. FPC* (Court of Appeals for the District of Columbia Circuit, No. 71-2012) decided November 9, 1973. In view of the usual dependence of thermal plants upon navigable streams (or their tributaries) for the necessary cooling water, a finding in favor of Commission jurisdiction would have had nationwide implications. The opinion contains a comprehensive analysis of the legislative background and intent of the 1920 Act.

[d]See *Scenic Hudson Preservation Conference v. FPC*, 354 F.2d 608 (2nd Circuit, 1966).

[e]*Udall v. FPC*, 387 U.S. 428 (1967).

[f]See *Greene County Planning District v. FPC*, 455 F.2d 412 (2nd Circuit, 1972).

depreciated net investment, less certain other amounts still in dispute. Thus, as project licenses for developed hydroelectric sites reach maturity the significance of FPC authority reemerges. As the Commission approached its 50th anniversary it was confronted with the task of determining the disposition of no less than 70 hydroelectric projects in the ensuing five-year period. Unable to accomplish this task on schedule (it has been complicated by the required preparation of environmental impact statements), the Commission has resorted to annual extensions as permitted in the 1920 Act.

Congress recognized the significance of collecting and disseminating information, to assist state commissions in the discharge of their responsibilities, and to provide a basis for comparative analysis of industry performance. The Commission was authorized "To make investigations . . . concerning the utilization of the water resources of any region . . . concerning the location, capacity, development costs, and relation to markets of power sites . . ." (16 USC 797(a)). We submit that "water resources" can be interpreted to include the use of any water for power production purposes. (Elsewhere in the legislation the Commission's licensing jurisdiction is restricted by notions of navigability.)

Considering the need for water for cooling purposes, the section covers almost the full scope of generating requirements now in use. Thus, utilizing its authority under that Section the Commission could conduct regional siting investigations. The Commission was encouraged to cooperate with "other agencies of State or National Governments" and "to make public from time to time the information secured hereunder and to provide for the publication of its reports and investigations in such form and manner as may be best adapted for public information and use."

This notion that the Commission is to serve as the collector and disseminator of information useful to other federal and state agencies (including state public utility commissions), while working closely with such agencies, is a recurrent one throughout the Act. Applicants for hydroelectric licenses, apart from the information requirements specified in the Act, are to submit "such additional information as the commission may require" (16 USC 802(c)).

With the expansion, in 1935, of the Commission's rate and accounting authority, its information and cooperative responsibilities were increased correspondingly. The Commission, *sua sponte* or at the request of a state commission, "may investigate and determine the cost of the production or transmission of electric energy by means of facilities under the jurisdiction of the Commission in cases where the Commission does not have the authority to establish a rate governing the sale of such energy" (16 USC 824e(b)).

New Initiatives

Any matter arising under the 1935 Act may be referred to a joint board composed of members of the Commission and of the utility commissions of affected states (16 USC 824h(a)). Further, "The Commission *shall* make available to the several state commissions such information and reports as may be of assistance in state regulation of public utilities" (16 USC 824h(c) (emphasis in original)).

Upon the receipt of a complaint the Commission may conduct any investigation it deems appropriate (16 USC 825e)); at any time it "may investigate any facts, conditions, practices or matters which [the Commission] may find necessary or proper in the discharge of its functions and "publish or make available to state commissions information concerning any such subject" (16 USC 825f(a)). It also has the power to perform any and all acts necessary or proper to carry out the objectives of the Federal Power Act (16 USC 825h). It is clear that the Commission has broad authority to secure information and make reports concerning all aspects of industry activity (16 USC 825j).

In carrying out its responsibility to collect from public utilities (and disseminate to the public) information relevant to the achievement of the Act's public interest objectives, the Commission should require each utility to file annually both ten-year demand projections and planned capacity solutions (by type, size, and general location). This information would then serve as the predicate for regional site investigations. It would seem preferable for the FPC to perform this function through the joint board mechanism, in cooperation with the state commissions within each region. Some state statutes—such as New York's—explicitly recognize the local agency's ability to participate on such boards. Most state statutes are silent, leaving open the possibility of such participation.

The joint board mechanism would give all interested parties a single forum in which to debate and settle upon appropriate sites for a defined future period, free of the "blackout" syndrome that surrounds every licensing case. Subsequently, when a license application is filed with an agency like the Atomic Energy Commission, it could treat the prior siting determination as a prima facie resolution of that issue (permitting only the introduction of newly discovered information) and concentrate on those issues most in keeping with its expertise. It would also seem appropriate to resolve the need question on a regional basis within the confines of the joint board regional hearing mechanism.

The Federal Power Commission could, through imaginative use of the authority which long has remained buried in the Federal Power Act, serve as a significant catalyst in securing more reasoned siting, even though its licensing authority extends only to hydroelectric projects. At a minimum, Federal Power Commission exposure of the underlying problems of financing and resource waste should stimulate cooperative planning efforts. Although we recommend that demand and site projection reports be required annually, a Federal Power Commission regional hearing could not realistically be conducted except over a several-year cycle. But the imposition of the reporting requirement would offer an opportunity for an early public debate over a utility's expansion plan. The sooner the debate begins the more likely that the siting decision reached will have carefully considered opposing views. Construction delays may thereby be lessened, although citizen opposition has not proven to be a significant cause of delay.

At a minimum, any agency that now exercises siting jurisdiction should make possible early public involvement in the decision making process by requiring the filing of "skeletal" applications two years prior to the filing of the detailed completed application. The skeletal filing would identify the type, size, and location of the contemplated facility without necessarily giving precise design specifications. The application could then be circulated to all utilities within the region to determine its consistency with the needs of others. Where another utility recognizes an opportunity for cooperation but declines to coordinate its future plans with those of the applicant, its own subsequent application would be looked upon with an initial negative predisposition.

This procedure will at least give smaller utilities (which often are not informed of joint participation efforts until plans have been committed) an opportunity to avoid the inherent wasteful consequences of isolated action. Moreover, it would facilitate local land use planning, which is often frustrated by a lack of information about utility expansion plans. When a detailed application is subsequently filed, the applicant should be required to demonstrate how approval of its proposal would further the objective of securing an economic, nonwasteful power supply for the area.

Moreover, the application should be required to be a complete filing. For example, where transmission facilities are at issue the utility should be required to disclose its full, ultimate plan and not simply an isolated stub line that it knows will be extended and integrated into its overall network. It is an abdication of regulatory responsibility for a commission to authorize a segment of a proposal (for example, part of a transmission grid, one circuit of an eventual double circuit line, or the first of multiple generation units) thereby "ruling out" any future exercise of judgment. The public is entitled to the long term picture before resources are committed.

To encourage public participation, actual hearings should be held, at least in part, in the area to be affected by a generating plant or transmission line. Further, in an effort to remove some of the economic obstacles that presently obstruct public participation, commissions should scrutinize transcript costs (which often exceed $200 per day) and, where possible, should have that function performed by public officials on a nominal fee basis. For example, the Wisconsin Public Service Commission, realizing that accessibility to transcripts is a necessity if participation is to be meaningful, freely supplies a copy to each party, including intervenors. Finally, commissions should search their authority for ways in which to ease the difficulty caused by the cost of expert witnesses who are indispensible to an effective presentation.

Commissions are usually free to hire outside consultants. Where an intervenor's expertise contributes to the development of a full record, the witness is in fact discharging an obligation that properly rests with the staff of the Commission.[g] In these circumstances use of consultant funds to reimburse the intervenor would seem most appropriate. There is little danger that this arrangement would be misused, since the determination to reimburse would be made at the end of the proceeding, based on the intervenor's contribution. Thus, an intervenor would not be assured of reimbursement for a frivolous presentation.

Rate Authority

Under the 1920 Act the Federal Power Commission was given rate authority over licensees, the authority to fix the net investment in a project (important for "recapture" or licensing to another licensee), to fix depreciation rates, and to establish amortization accounts. The Commission was to exercise its limited rate authority only until such time as a state commission assumed responsibility.[h] However, experience during the 1920-1935 period showed the need for a more comprehensive federal regulatory scheme.

In 1927 the Supreme Court held that state authority to regulate electric rates was limited to matters of local distribution and could not extend to interstate sales for resale (interutility wholesale sales).[i] Since FPC authority over rates under the 1920 Act was limited to hydroelectric power and even then only in the absence of state regulation, a regulatory gap became evident (16 USC 812, 813). In addition, a Federal Trade Commission study of corporate abuses found that there was a need for regulatory oversight over interlocking directorates, mergers, acquisitions and the issuance of securities. It became apparent that if the nation was to be assured an adequate, reliable and efficient supply of electricity, mechanisms had to be developed to encourage industry cooperative efforts. Congress responded, in 1935, with the enactment of Part II of the Federal Power Act.

The Commission was given comprehensive rate regulatory authority by two Sections of the 1935 Act. Section 205 (16 USC 824d) is concerned with new rate filings, and Section 206 (16 USC 824e) with rates which are already in effect. Under Section 205, utilities are required to prefile rate changes for wholesale sales. Upon receipt of a rate filing the Commission has two options. It can permit the rate change to become effective immediately, in which case the utility can begin to charge at the new rates. Or, the Commission can suspend the rate filing for a maximum of five months. During the suspension period the Commission will analyze the filing and may hold an adversary proceeding to determine whether the rates are just and reasonable.

---

[g]See *Scenic Hudson Preservation Society v. FPC*, 354 F.2d 608 (CA 2, 1965) certiorari denied 384 U.S. 941 and *Office of the United Church of Christ v. FCC*, 359 F.2d 994 (CADC, 1966), and 425 F.2d 543 (CADC, 1969).

[h]16 USC 812 and 813.

[i]*Public Utility Commission of Rhode Island v. Attleboro Steam Electric Company*, 273 U.S. 83.

Interested persons (e.g., customers of the utility) may contest the increase. If the Commission does not complete its deliberations by the end of the maximum five-month suspension period, the rate becomes effective. The important distinction, however, is that the direct result of the suspension order is to permit the Commission, should it ultimately determine that the rates are excessive, to direct the utility to make refunds to its customers. If the Commission had allowed the rates to go into effect without suspension it could not order refunds but would be limited to prospective relief. Rates, charges, and conditions of service are to be just and reasonable and are not to grant any undue preference or advantage to any users or to provide undue differences between either localities or classes of service. If the rates proposed or placed into effect by a utility fail to satisfy the statutory standards, the Commission has authority to fix appropriate rates.

Rate Base Regulation

The typical electric rate proceeding is divided into two parts. Regulatory agencies (both the Federal Power Commission and state utility commissions) first determine how much a utility will be allowed to earn, or what the utility's "revenue requirement" will be. In the second phase of the procedure, regulators must approve rate schedules designed to achieve the designated required revenue.

Regulatory attention has historically been focused on the first phase or rate base regulation. Regulators first estimate the rate base (or net investment) of the utility and then determine the maximum allowable rate of return on that investment. That amount, in addition to operating expenses and taxes, constitutes the utilities revenue requirement.

The return available for distribution to stockholders is a function of the size of the utility's rate base (ordinarily its net investment or the depreciated original cost of its capital equipment) and the level of its allowed rate of return. While theoretically a utility's revenues can be increased either by increasing its rate of return or its rate base, a utility would not have an incentive to add to its rate base unless its allowed rate of return was greater than the cost of capital needed to expand that base. (In so stating we have chosen to ignore managerial incentives to expand for the sake of expansion.)

It has been contended by citizen group intervenors that present rate base regulation supplies a strong incentive to capital expansions or "gold-plating"—the so-called A-J effect. The paramount decision making consideration, they argue, is not the ultimate social utility of the particular investment but whether the return to stockholders will be increased. For example, in situations where common transmission facilities can serve two or more utilities considerations of environmental, social and economic efficiency operate in favor of joint facilities. Rate of return considerations may, however, encourage duplication.

Utilities that logically should concentrate on the ultimate distribution function (purchasing all or nearly all of their power requirements from larger, more efficient generators), are encouraged to enter the production phase themselves. If, following an investment, a utility is unable to realize its allowed (and contemplated) rate of return it should easily be able to secure commission approval for additional revenues through rate increases. Usually rate increases are designed so as not to drive customers to competing energy suppliers.

The utility is thus encouraged to take business risks (such as the overexpansion of plant capacity) that a highly competitive firm would be unlikely to take. It can expand, and should it be left with excess capacity its rate schedules could be revised to promote consumption by offering discounts to consumers who enjoy energy alternatives. Any revenue deficiency would be recouped by exacting higher prices from locked-in consumers.[j]

Although the Federal Power Commission has been cautious in adopting innovative rate regulatory approaches, its conservatism is not required by law. Neither the governing statutory provisions nor Court interpretations require that rate regulation be of a static nature. The Supreme Court has freed the Federal Power Commission from restrictive adherence to rigid formulas. It has adopted an "end result" test which measures the rate order against the statutorily provided general standards of fairness and reasonableness. Moreover, the Court has recently indicated that the Commission is obliged to consider broader social questions under its obligation to protect the public interest. The Commission has the responsibility to protect future as well as present consumer and public interests, and may employ price functionally.[k]

Thus the Court has made it clear that

> The Constitution does not bind rate making bodies to the service of any single formula or combination of formulas. Agencies to whom this legislative power has been delegated are free, within the ambit of their statutory authority, to make pragmatic adjustments which may be called for by particular circumstances.[l]

While this and subsequent decisions were concerned with analysis of the Natural Gas Act, the similarity of the statutory language applicable to

---

[j]Alfred Kahn has concluded that this tendency to become capital intensive results in: (1) the resistance of utilities to implementation of peak pricing policies; (2) a willingness to maintain a high percentage of standby reserves; (3) reluctance to coordinate investment on a regional basis; (4) resistance to capital saving technology; (5) reluctance to lease facilities in lieu of self-construction (e.g., to purchase capacity in lieu of self-generation); (6) adherence to excessively high standards of reliability; (7) lack of bargaining incentive in dealings with equipment suppliers; and (8) willingness to promote load growth at rates, if necessary, that fail to recover incremental costs. *The Economics of Regulation*, Vol. II, New York: John Wiley, 1971, pp. 50-54.

[k]The reader interested in reviewing the earlier and more restrictive judicial pronouncements should see *Smyth v. Ames*, 169 U.S. 466 (1898); *Missouri ex rel Southwestern Bell Telephone Co. v. PUC*, 262 U.S. 276, 287 (1923); and *McCardle v. Indianapolis Water Company*, 272 U.S. 400 (1926).

[l]*FPC v. Natural Gas Pipeline Co.*, 315 U.S. 575, 586 (1942).

electric and natural gas proceedings makes these holdings relevant. It should be noted that the electric power industry involves outright monopolies that are regulated on a cost basis. Neither the total absence of intraindustry competition nor the requirement that rates be cost based is as clear in the case of the natural gas industry.

The decision to release the FPC from obedience to a particular formula was quickly followed by the development of the "end result" test announced in the *Hope* case.[m]

> Congress ... has provided no formula by which the "just and reasonable" rate is to be determined. It has not filled in the details of the general prescription. It has not expressed in a specific rule, the fixed principle of "just and reasonable." ... Under the statutory standard of just and reasonable it is the result reached not the method employed which is controlling.

The lower federal courts interpreted *Hope* narrowly at first; they did not construe it as permitting a total departure from rate base regulation.[n] However, the potential for rate setting flexibility was eventually recognized.[o]

The Federal Power Commission first departed from the rate base method in *Permian Basin Area Rate Cases*,[p] basing rates for natural gas producers on area rates, rather than on individual production costs.[q] The Supreme Court concluded that

> rate making agencies are not bound to the service of any single regulatory formula; they are permitted, unless their statutory authority otherwise plainly indicates, to make the pragmatic adjustments which may be called for by particular circumstances.[r] ... [The Court reiterat[ed] that] the breadth and complexity of the Commission's responsibilities demand that it be given every reasonable opportunity to formulate methods of regulation appropriate for the solution of its intensely practical difficulties.[s]

[m]*FPC v. Hope Natural Gas Co.*, 320 U.S. 591, 600, 602 (1943).

[n]See *Pennsylvania Water & Power Co., v. FPC*, 193 F.2d 230, 242 (D.C. Cir., 1951), aff'd. 343 U.S. 414 and *Safe Harbor Water Power Corp. v. FPC*, 179 F.2d 179 (3rd Cir., 1949).

[o]See *City of Detroit v. FPC*, 230 F.2d 810, 813-814 (1955).

[p]390 U.S. 747 (1967).

[q]390 U.S. 747 (1967). It must be emphasized, however, that the rates in the *Permian* case were still cost based. Indeed, the Supreme Court was aware of the extensive cost data collected by the Commission. In suggesting the possibility of departing from rate base regulation we do not mean to imply that a Commission is free to ignore costs in determining a utility's revenue requirements.

[r]*Id.* at 777-778.

[s]*Id.* at 790.

Thus it is apparent that the Commission and its state counterparts can apply rate base regulation functionally and use innovative economic incentives. Any approach must recognize that the utility's property may not be confiscated. The utility must be afforded an opportunity to earn a just and reasonable return. This flexibility notwithstanding, the FPC in its regulation of the wholesale rates of electric utilities, and state utility commissions in the regulation of rates charged the ultimate consumer, have strictly adhered to traditional rate base methodology. The FPC determines the rate base by calculating the original cost of facilities and subtracting the depreciation accumulated up to the test year upon which rates are predicated. Three basic procedures are discernible in state rate base methodologies. (There is now some move toward permitting adjustments to the test year data upon which a utility's revenue requirements are determined to account for known future changes. By rule, the New York Public Service Commission permits recognition of such future changes by test year adjustments.)

A group of twelve states (*Smyth v. Ames* states) bases the rate base calculation on an assessment of "fair value" variously defined as reproduction, replacement cost, or present value.[t] A second group of fifteen states, uses original cost depreciated, book cost, net investment and the prudent investment test as historically understood.[u] Finally, a group of eighteen states following *FPC v. Hope*, has abandoned strict adherence to any particular formula while not discarding the rate base method in principle.[v]

---

[t] *Arizona (Arizona Corp. Comm. v. Arizona Water Co.*, 85 Ariz. 198, 335 P. 2d 412); *Delaware (In re Diamond State Telephone Co.*, 46 Del. 203, 206-207, 113 A.2d 437 (1955)); *Illinois, (Illinois Bell Telephone Co. v. Illinois Commerce Commission*, 414 Ill. 275, 111 NE 2d 329 (1953)); *Indiana (Public Service Commission v. Indiana Bell Telephone Co.*, 235 Ind. 115, 130 NE 2d 467 (1955); *Maryland* (Md. Code Ann. 78-69); *Missouri (State v. Public Service Commission*, 308 S.W. 2d 704 (1957)); *Montana (State v. Public Service Commission*, 131 Mont. 104, 308 P.2d 633, 637 (1957); *New Mexico* (compare *State Corp. Commission v. Mountain State Telephone Co.*, 58 N.M. 260, 270 P.2d 685 (1954) and *Moryston v. Public Service Commission*, 76 N.M. 146, 402 P.2d 840 (1966)); *North Carolina (State v. Piedmont Natural Gas Co.*, 254 N.C. 536, 119 S.E. 2d 469 (1961); *Ohio (Ohio Edison Co. v. Public Utility Commission*, 173 Ohio 448; 184 N.E. 2d 70 (1962)); *Pennsylvania (Scranton v. Scranton Steam Heat Co.*, 405 Pa. 397, 401-402, 176 A.2d 86 (1961)); and *Texas (Railroad Commission v. Houston Natural Gas Corp.*, 155 Tex. 502, 522, 289 S.W. 2d 559 (1956)).

[u] *Alabama; Alaska; Arkansas* (see *Acme Brick Co. v. Public Service Commission*, 299 S.W. 2d 208 (1957)); *California (cf: Application of California Water and Telephone Co.*, 65 Cal. P.U.C. 281 (1966); *San Francisco v. Public Utility Commission*, 98 Cal. Rep. 286, 490 P.2d 798 (1971)); *Idaho (Idaho Underground Water Users Ass'n. v. Idaho Power Co.*, 89 Id. 147, 404 P.2d 859, 866 (1965)); *Maine; Michigan (Michigan Bell Telephone Co. v. Public Service Commission*, 332 Mich. 7, 50 N.W. 2d 826 (1952)); *Nevada* (see *Public Service Commission v. Ely Light & Power Co.*, 80 Nev. 312, 393 P.2d 305, 309 (1964); *North Dakota; Oregon; Vermont; Virginia; West Virginia; Wisconsin;* and *Wyoming.*

[v] *Colorado (Public Utility Commission v. Northwest*, 168 Col. 154, 173 (1969)); *Connecticut (Norton Water Co. v. Public Utility Commission*, 24 Conn. Super. 441, 193 A.2d 724, 726 (1962)); *Florida (Jacksonville Gas Corp. v. Railroad & Public Utilities Commission*, 50 So. 2d 887 (1951)); *Hawaii (In Re Application of Hawaiian Electric Co., Ltd.*, 42 Hawaii 233, 238 (1957)); *Iowa (Davenport Water Co. v. State Commerce*

The Supreme Court has acknowledged that a company is entitled to a fair return on the property it employs for the public convenience. Without that return, a confiscatory taking results. However, the just and reasonable standard goes to the result reached and not to the method employed in setting rates. The Constitution as interpreted by the courts does not require any particular formula so long as the formula employed does not result in an unconstitutional taking.

The constitutional standard applies to the confiscation of property; it does not prescribe any particular return and in fact it is clear that any rate of return within the so-called zone of reasonableness will be sustained. This leads to at least one possibility for innovation in rate base regulation. If regulatory commissions can establish ranges can they not also permit the utility to achieve a higher return if its operations achieve certain standards?

Thus a commission seeking a particular objective could use the return formula to supply rewards and penalties for utility performance. For example, the Commission could fix the range of return at between 7 and 9 percent allowing the utility a base of 8 percent. For each positive step taken by the utility toward the achievement of the desired objective, it would be rewarded by an increase in return (up to a maximum of 9 percent). For each negative step taken by the utility its allowed return would be adjusted down until a minimum return of not less than 7 percent were reached. Where the utility earns a right to a higher return under such a formula, it could be permitted to file new rate schedules designed to secure the permissible added revenues, which would be accepted without suspension thus relieving the utility of the fear of triggering a rate case. Conversely, where a revenue decline is appropriate the utility should be obliged to file appropriate tariff revisions. Much the same procedure could be used to penalize unsatisfactory customer service.

The point is simply that the FPC and state commissions generally, without in any way departing from traditional principles of rate of return regulation, can establish standards of performance (for example, standards of

Commission, 190 N.W. 2d 583, 591 (1971)); *Kansas* (*Southwestern Bell Telephone Co. v. State Corporation Commission*, 192 Kan. 39, 65, 386 P.2d 515 (1963)); *Kentucky* (*Lexington v. Public Service Commission*, 249 S.W. 2d 760 (1952)); *Louisiana* (*Morehouse Natural Gas Co. v. Public Service Commission*, 242 La. 985, 140 So. 2d 646, 651-652 (1962)); *Massachusetts* (*New England Telephone and Telegraph Co. v. Department of Public Utilities*, 331 Mass. 604, 121 N.E. 2d 896, 903 (1954)); *Mississippi* (*Southern Bell Telephone Co. v. Public Service Commission*, 237 Miss. 157, 113 So. 2d 622, 644 (1959)); *New Hampshire* (*Granite State Alarm Inc. v. New England Telephone & Telegraph*, 117 N.H. 235, 279 A.2d 595, 597 (1971)); *New Jersey* (*State v. N.J. Bell Telephone Co.*, 30 N.J. 16, 152 A.2d 35, 42-43 (1959)); *New York* (*N.Y. Telephone Co. v. Public Service Commission*, 309 N.Y. 569, 132 N.E. 2d 847, 850 (1956); *Oklahoma* (*Southwestern Bell Telephone Co. v. State*, 204 Okla. 225, 230 P.2d 260, 265 (1951)); *Rhode Island* (*Massachusetts Electric Co. v. Kennelly*, 88 R.I. 56, 68, 143 A.2d 709 (1958)); *South Dakota* (*Application of Northwest Bell Telephone Co.*, 78 S.D. 15, 26, 98 N.W. 2d 170 (1959)); *Utah* (*Utah Power & Light Co. v. Public Service Commission*, 107 Utah 155, 183, 152 P.2d 542 (1944)); and *Washington* (*State ex rel. Pacific Telephone & Telegraph Co. v. Department of Public Service*, 19 Wash. 2d 200, 233-234, 142 P.2d 498 (1943)).

environmental performance) and establish a sliding scale rate of return to provide incentives for the desired utility responses. There are no constitutional or statutory restrictions as long as the utility is permitted to earn, at a minimum, the bottom rate of return within the zone of reasonableness range.

There is a second way in which traditional regulatory activities can be used to counteract the promotional aspects of rate base regulation. Commissions traditionally have had the authority to determine what types of investment may properly be included in a utility's rate base. Hence, if a utility is investing in plant capacity that will ultimately erode company earnings, the Commission could find that the investment is imprudent and deny it rate base treatment. Such could also be the case where the utility ignored integration and coordination possibilities with neighboring systems in favor of wholly owned self-generation. At a minimum, if the utility denied itself the benefits of economies of scale that it could have realized by joining in partnership with a neighbor on a larger facility the Commission should be free to discount from rate base the excess capacity payments.

We recognize that rate base determinations are almost always made after the fact—after capital has been committed. And since the investment has been dedicated to utility service, it may be impossible at that stage to exclude it totally from rate base. A commission should have greater flexibility, at least to exclude "excess" costs, if it announces its benchmark standards in advance. Commissions should be encouraged to do this as a means both of dampening inefficient growth and promoting desirable integration.

Lastly, there must be sensitivity to the realities that confront a utility when it faces the question of constructing nonrevenue producing pollution abatement equipment. By nonrevenue producing we mean only that the equipment does not increase the utility's installed capacity and therefore its ability to expand service. To the extent that the cost of the facility is included in the utility's rate base it is of course revenue producing as soon as further rate relief is obtained. Ordinarily if a utility can earn more than its cost of capital the incentive would be to add the capital equipment, particularly if the commission will permit the utility to earn interest during construction as the FPC allows for certain expenditures for research and development. Where those expenditures are to be recouped within one year they are treated as an operating expense. Where the recoupment period is longer and the research and development is being undertaken by the utility itself, the utility is allowed to treat the expenditures as construction work in progress and is permitted to earn interest during construction (at a rate somewhat below the authorized return). Where the research and development funds are contributed to projects undertaken by others (e.g., Edison Electric Institute) the utility would be permitted to amortize (expense) over a five-year period and such amounts could be treated as operating expenses should there be a rate case. In any event, no interest during construction would be realized.

There are, however, additional considerations that confront a utility faced with the choice of installing expensive pollution abatement equipment or continuing to use high priced fuel. For example, assume that a utility burns natural gas for boiler fuel and that, in view of its scarcity, the price of gas goes up. If, as is likely, the utility has a fuel adjustment clause it has the option of continuing to purchase gas (assuming its continued availability at the higher price) or switching to an alternative fuel and installing pollution abatement equipment. If the latter option is chosen it would add to its rate base but would realize that benefit only after a new rate determination. If the utility is already earning a reasonable return (or more) it may not be anxious to precipitate a rate case. Moreover, it may not wish to confront the regulatory lag inherent in the filing of new rate levels.

Conversely, in view of the automatic fuel adjustment clause, the utility can continue its use of natural gas, immediately pass the extra costs on thereby avoiding the prejudice of regulatory lag, and avoid an inquiry into its rates. If the least social cost production technique is not selected, this would result in the inferior use of a depleting resource.[w] The problem is an acute one. In 1972, 4 trillion cubic feet of natural gas was used as boiler fuel for the generation of electricity in the United States with almost half of that amount so consumed in four southwestern states (Arkansas, Louisiana, Oklahoma, and Texas).[x] This particular problem could be dealt with by giving the FPC end use jurisdiction over the intrastate, as well as the interstate, consumption of natural gas, or by pricing *all* gas at marginal social cost.

In addition to the incentive supplied by interest during construction, it may be possible to single out certain types of capital commitments (pollution abatement, for example), for specialized treatment. Tax free pollution control bonds are an example of such specialized treatment. A commission could establish a weighted rate of return which in effect allows a greater percentage return on capital invested for pollution abatement purposes. This would favor capital solutions rather than fuel substitutions. Similarly, commissions might

---

[w]In speaking of "inferior use" we are not speaking strictly in economic terms. We recognize that in traditional economic theory if a buyer is willing to outbid all others for the available supply of a product, the use ultimately made of that product is not considered inferior—indeed, is irrelevant. We could readily accept that principle if natural gas were sold at its marginal cost. It is not. Instead the seller of natural gas rolls-in all of his costs and comes up with a rather uniform average price. Under this procedure there can be no assurance that natural gas will not be put to inferior uses in either the traditional economic sense or the more common lay understanding. It would seem more appropriate to adopt marginal cost pricing as the rule and deviate from it (to avoid excess earnings to the natural gas company) by applying the rules of inverse price elasticity. This would lead to larger discounts (away from the marginal cost) for inelastic consumers and smaller discounts for those consumers who enjoy greater flexibility. Included within the latter group would be those utilities which can burn substitute fuels. As long as current pricing distortions are permitted to exist in the case of natural gas, however, it is appropriate to be concerned with inferior uses in the lay sense.

[x]American Gas Association, *Gas Facts*, 1972.

agree to an automatic readjustment of revenues to reflect the expansion of a utility's rate base as a result of such investments, while giving assurances that such increased revenues would not be considered in determining whether the utility is earning excessive revenues. It could agree that the allowance of such additional revenues would not subject the utility to a general reexamination of its earnings level. Of course each of these incentive systems could be the subject of abuse (particularly the allowance of a weighted rate of return) and before the Commission acts, it should either announce expenditure guidelines or provide a mechanism for abbreviated preinvestment review.

Rate Design

Although the law imposes the burden of justifying a rate design on its proponent (the utility), utilities have not been forced to accept that responsibility. Many regulatory commissions have viewed their task to be at an end once they have determined the utility's revenue requirement. The actual design of rates to produce those revenues has been left largely to the discretion of utility management. But the recent failures of utilities to earn previously authorized earnings has resulted in the need for recurring rate increase filings. State utility commissions are now exhibiting a new interest in rate design and in particular in the promotional implications of declining block structures. In response to citizen intervention, at least thirteen commissions or utilities (in California, Colorado, District of Columbia, Florida, Maryland, Michigan, Missouri, Nevada, New York, Utah, Vermont, Virginia, and Wisconsin), have taken action directed at "flattening" the slope of declining block rates or imposing a premium for peak period consumption. See the 1972 and 1973 Opinions of the New York Public Service Commission with regard to rate applications of Consolidated Edison (Opinion Nos. 72-6 and 73-31), the May 25, 1973 order of the Michigan Public Service Commission (Case No. U-4257) directing Detroit Edison to analyze in depth the growth and resulting economic implications of its rate structure and the August 8, 1974 decision of the Wisconsin Public Service Commission (Case No. 2-U-7423, Madison Gas and Electric Co.) adopting the principles of peak load pricing.

In examining the potential impact of the FPC on rate design it must be recognized that only 10 percent of the revenues realized by investor-owned utilities are the result of wholesale transactions subject to federal rate jurisdiction. Nevertheless we focus on rate design at the federal level. States may hesitate to unilaterally reform rate designs, for fear of placing the utilities within their jurisdiction at a competitive disadvantage. A demonstration of leadership at the national level seems appropriate to encourage the adoption of innovative designs.

Consider the Federal Power Commission's responsibility for assuring an abundant supply of electricity throughout the United States "with the greatest possible economy and with regard to the proper utilization and conservation of natural resources" (16 USC 824a(a)). "Proper utilization and conservation of natural resources" recognizes that the ability of the environment to accommodate power plants and transmission lines is not infinite; indeed, that the availability of suitable sites is limited. "With the greatest possible economy" emphasizes the need to resist inefficient expansion. Considering these objectives it is not unreasonable to contend that the FPC has the responsibility to analyze in depth current cost trends and pricing practices, perhaps on a regional basis. Innovative action by the FPC on current rate structure problems, even with respect to the limited tariffs under its jurisdiction, should have a significant effect on state commissions. The states often lack the resources necessary to assess the legitimacy of economic and environmental arguments in favor of rate restructuring.

The FPC also has the ability to influence the rate activities of Interior Department power marketing agencies directly. (For a discussion of the federal marketing agencies see Appendix C.) It must approve the rates of those agencies. The FPC has routinely accepted and approved the rates filed by Bonneville and the other federal marketing agencies; it does no more than raise an occasional question. Considering differences in consumption patterns between regions served by such federal agencies and other parts of the nation it is clear that federal marketing practices have influenced consumption patterns. One need only look at the level of industrial activity concentrated in the Bonneville marketing area.

The problem with Bonneville's rates, and those of Interior marketing agencies generally, may not be so much structure (Bonneville does endeavor to promote high load factor off peak industrial consumption) as with price levels. The Bonneville system is to "be operated for the benefit of the general public, and particularly of domestic and rural customers.[y] If the public is being asked to subsidize industrial consumption, the extent of that subsidy must be weighed against the benefits ultimately derived.[z] In the case of Bonneville's industrial sales, which are in the main made on an interruptible basis, the subsidy would appear to be twofold. First, its customers enjoy the benefit of rates designed to recover the cost of federal capital, which costs less than comparable private capital. Second, at present customers (all customers, not just industrial users), are not paying for any negative social externalities of power production and transmission.[aa]

---

[y]16 USC 832c(b).

[z]According to its 1972 Annual Report, Bonneville sold in excess of 63 billion kilowatt hours of electricity, approximately 60 billion of which was sold in the Pacific Northwest area. Of the latter total, sales to publicly owned utilities, privately owned utilities and industrial consumers were, respectively, 23.2, 13.6 and 22.6 billion kwh. By far the major segment of the industrial sales went to the aluminum industry. The rest was consumed largely by chemical and metallurgical firms.

[aa]The legislative history of the Bonneville Act is filled with references that Congress intended for Bonneville's rates to be "yardsticks" for the rates charged by the privately owned utilities in the region. The yardstick principle was mentioned in conjunction with the argument for public control of the area's significant water power resources. An interesting question concerns the scope of the "yardstick principle." Is the principle to

Congress clearly intended preferential treatment through reduced electric rates for rural and domestic customers. However, it is open to question whether nonpreference industrial customers (whether they purchase directly from Bonneville or indirectly through a preference customer on peak) should receive a similar subsidy. Present financing practices will underprice electricity and, in view of the apparent price elasticity of industrial consumption, stimulate it. Failing to assess the full social cost of service will result in price distortions and consumption inefficiencies. The Bonneville enabling legislation (as is generally true of federal marketing legislation) presumes that prices will be set to recoup all costs.

Department of the Interior marketing agencies can do more than set prices charged the ultimate consumers they serve. These agencies can also influence the rate structures of their wholesale customers—that is, their utility customers, who purchase for resale. For example, Bonneville distributed 23.2 billion kwh to publicly owned utility systems and 13.6 billion kwh to privately owned utility systems in the Pacific Northwest area in fiscal year 1972. Outside the Northwest it distributed almost 3 billion kwh to public and private utility systems. Bonneville is required to precondition its sales in order to insure that resales by its utility customers "to the ultimate consumer shall be at rates which are reasonable and nondiscriminatory" (16 USC 832d(a)).

If resale customers of Bonneville are distributing electricity pursuant to declining block rates, and if those rates are prejudicial to initial block or residential customers, Bonneville has ample authority to demand a corrective restructuring as a condition to the supplying of this relatively inexpensive federal power. Indeed, Bonneville can prescribe rate design standards to be followed by its utility customers. Such action by Bonneville can be expected to have a psychological impact on state utility commissions. The FPC can demonstrate the necessary leadership when called upon to review Bonneville's rates.

Utilities, in an effort to improve their load factors, often endeavor to promote off peak usage through rate design. For example, those utilities that experience a summer peak may seek to promote electric heat through rate design. Sometimes a separate rate schedule is applied to all electric homes and sometimes a single tariff is divided into blocks which offer an incentive to the consumer to choose electric heating. Generally, the availability of off-peak promotional rates is not dependent upon the satisfaction of prescribed minimum insulation standards, although insulation would reduce energy consumption. (See David Large, *Hidden Waste*, Conservation Foundation, 1973.) The FPC could easily correct this shortcoming by aiming an educational campaign at state commissions and by influencing (if only indirectly) the rate schedules of wholesale power from Interior marketing agencies.

apply only to rates charged for electric power or as well to general utility operations? Congressional preoccupation with rates no doubt is explained by the fact that in the 1930's rates were considered the key benchmark of utility performance. Today, as new social concerns assume prominence, it may be appropriate to widen the yardstick concept.

Finally, the FPC, and each state commission, should require every rate applicant to analyze the impact of its proposed rate design on consumption patterns. It will not be possible for Commission staffs or citizen group intervenors to address rate design questions in every case. Utilities must begin to consider such implications themselves. As a complimentary measure the FPC should extend its reporting and analysis to the collection of the data essential for formulating responsible rate designs including, for example, specific data on consumption practices (such as bill frequency analyses).

One of the more serious problems confronting state utility commissions is their inability to assess cost trends. The Federal Power Act repeatedly confers upon the FPC the full authority to examine all matters touching upon the cost of generating, transmitting and distributing electricity.

Congress no doubt was aware of the importance of such assessments not only to the FPC but to state commissions, most of which lack the resources and even the jurisdictional competence to undertake this required analysis. Hence, the FPC repeatedly is reminded of its authority and responsibility to collect and analyze cost information, to publish such information and otherwise to assist state commissions.

At a minimum it is open to the Federal Power Commission to undertake a comprehensive analysis of cost questions and to cooperate with state utility commissions through the mechanism of regional hearings. It is often the case today that local utilities obtain power from plants located in another state. This is certainly common to utilities that are members of holding companies or which participate in regional pools. Assuming that a state commission had the resources and inclination to examine costs, jurisdictional problems might arise. All these problems, including that of resources, can be met by invocation of the federal-state joint board approach as contemplated by the Federal Power Act (16 USC 824h).

Use of that mechanism would have several advantages. It would permit several state commissions within a region, working in cooperation with the FPC, to examine cost and related rate questions that none could examine independently. This may be particularly important in determining elasticities and implementing innovative rate schedules at the distribution level. When environmentalists have urged the revision of declining block rates, utility and business interests have been quick to warn that the result would not be the curbing of inefficient consumption, but its relocation to the service area of a utility that maintains declining block charges. A regional approach to rate regulation could alleviate the problem.

Environmental and other social externalities do differ from region to region (but perhaps less drastically within a region). The regional assessment approach would not only allow a more comprehensive examination, but would also alleviate jurisdictional problems that might confront state commissions dealing with plants outside their regulatory authority. Most significantly, absent federal participation it is highly unlikely that the task of defining costs would be undertaken at all. The presence of federal participants would, moreover, help to assure more effective implementation of recommendations. As more attention is focused on the external or social costs of utility operations, one must ask the extent to which Commissions can consider these costs in rate design.

The body of relevant authority has been developed, in the main, on the natural gas side of the FPC's authority as it has struggled to develop a pricing system intended to stimulate adequate production, while preventing waste. In the *Hope* case the Supreme Court observed, somewhat gratuitously, that at least in the context of the Natural Gas Act, the Commission lacked "the power to fix rates which will disallow or discourage resales for industrial use." The Court viewed the authority to fix rates "so as to discourage particular uses" a "novel" doctrine of rate making which could not be invoked absent a statutory predicate. In his dissent Justice Frankfurter stated:

> Of course the statute is not concerned with abstract theories of rate making, but its very foundation is the "public interest," and the public interest is a texture of multiple strands. It includes more than contemporary investors and contemporary consumers. The needs to be served are not restricted to immediacy, and social as well as economic costs must be counted (320 U.S. at 627).

The more limited view of the *Hope* majority was to endure throughout most of the evolution of natural gas pricing with the early decisions emphasizing the need to restrict the Commission's rate making determinations strictly to economic considerations.[bb] In recent years, however, as it became apparent that pricing questions could not logically be severed from more general policy considerations, the Courts have been willing to sanction rate design flexibility. Thus in *Permian*, the Supreme Court observed:

> The Commission cannot confine its inquiries either to the computation of costs of service or to conjectures about the prospective responses of the capital market; it is instead obliged at each step of its regulatory process to assess the broad public interests entrusted to its protection by Congress. Accordingly the end result of the Commission's orders must be measured as much by the success with which they protect those interests as by the effectiveness with which they "maintain credit . . . and . . . attract capital."

[bb]For example, in *Alston Coal Co. v. FPC*, 137 F.2d 740, 741-742 (10th Cir., 1943), the Court held that the Commission could not justifiably fix "higher rates in order to prevent economic injury to competing fuels. The effect of a gas rate upon a competing fuel industry is not a factor which under the Act the Commission may consider in a proceeding for the establishment of a gas rate." And in *Detroit v. FPC*, 230 F.2d 810, 817 (D.C. Cir., 1955), the Commission was told that it could not base natural gas field prices on "consideration[s] of conservation." See also *Fuels Research Council, Inc. v. FPC*, 379 F.2d 842, 854 (7th Cir., 1967).

The Commission may, within this zone, employ price functionally in order to achieve relevant regulatory purposes; it may, in particular, take fully into account the probable consequences of a given price level for future programs of exploration and production. Nothing in the purposes or history of the Act forbids the Commission to require different prices for different sales, even if the distinctions are unrelated to quality, if these arrangements are "necessary or appropriate to carry out the provisions of this Act.' 15 USC 717o. We hold that the statutory "just and reasonable" standard permits the Commission to require differences in price for simultaneous sales of gas of identical quality, if it has permissibly found that such differences will effectively serve the regulatory purposes contemplated by Congress.[cc]

Just as *Hope*, by stipulating an "end result" test, freed the Commission from the need to adhere to any particular computational method of rate regulation, *Permian* appears to allow the same flexibility on issues of rate design. Further support for this view is to be found in the judicial approval of the Commission's second area rate order.[dd] Referring to the addition of incentive pricing features the Court observed:

We think that the need for dramatically increased production from Southern Louisiana justifies the non-cost factors added here, and that the FPC has power to include non-cost elements that reflect its assessment of the need to use price as a tool to influence such economic relations. These are propositions that apply generally to regulation of utilities and quasi-utilities.

* * * * *

At this point, we emphasize the fact that the Commission has justified the non-cost factors by reference to considerations that ostensibly affect not private but broad public interests.

If the future public need for natural gas may appropriately be considered in constructing a rate design, other public interests including protection of the environment, recoupment of social costs, and discouragement of wasteful consumption, may also be deemed appropriate by the Courts. This is particularly true for the Federal Power Act. To be sure the availability of natural gas reserves bears directly on natural gas customers while environmental concerns may be said to be somewhat more removed on the electric side. We submit however that those and other social concerns tend to impact the availability of adequate supplies of electricity. While the Natural Gas Act gives

---

[cc]390 U.S. 747, 791, 797-798.

[dd]*Southern Louisiana Area Rate Cases v. FPC*, 428 F.2d 407, 426-427 (5th Cir., 1970), cert. den. 400 U.S. 950.

the Commission broad investigative powers, only the Federal Power Act details Congressional concern for protection and promotion of the public interest (15 USC 717m).

Corporate Regulation and Pooling

In order to regulate the major corporate transactions of public utilities which were not within holding companies (and therefore not subject to Securities and Exchange Commission supervision) the 1935 Federal Power Act gave the FPC jurisdiction over mergers, acquisitions, property dispositions, security issues and interlocking directorates. The Act requires FPC approval for the sale, lease or disposition of facilities valued in excess of $50,000 which are subject to Commission jurisdiction; for the merger or consolidation of such facilities with those of another person; or for the acquisition of the securities of another public utility (16 USC 824c). Approval is to be granted if "the proposed disposition, consolidation, acquisition, or control [is] consistent with the public interest." The FPC may stipulate the conditions necessary to "secure the maintenance of adequate service and the coordination in the public interest of facilities subject to the jurisdiction of the Commission." This authority is not displaced by the assertion of equivalent jurisdiction at the state level.

The 1920 Act which specifies the Commission's licensing authority explicitly prohibits "combinations, agreements, arrangements, or understandings, express or implied, to limit the output of electrical energy, to restrain trade, or to fix, maintain, or increase prices for electrical energy or service" (16 USC 803(h)).

Commission jurisdiction over securities extends to those of a limited group of public utilities not regulated by state commissions. Approval is to be granted if the issuance is reasonably necessary or appropriate in the discharge of lawful utility activities, is in the public interest and will not result in the impairment of utility services (16 USC 824c).

Without Commission approval no person may hold an interlocking directorate, that is, serve as a director of more than one public utility, or of a public utility and of a firm authorized to underwrite or market utility securities, or of one which supplies electrical equipment to a public utility. To date the Commission has approved the majority of applications submitted by persons serving as directors of affiliated public utilities within a holding company system. It is common to find interlocking directorships between utilities and banks, as well as substantial stock under the control of banking institutions.[ee]

The FPC is directed to promote and encourage "the voluntary interconnection and coordination of facilities for the generation, transmission and sale of electric energy" in order to "assure an abundant supply of electric

---

[ee]See, *Commercial Banks and their Trust Activities, Emerging Influence on the American Economy*, a 1968 report prepared for the House Committee on Banking and Currency.

energy throughout the United States with the greatest possible economy and with regard to the proper utilization and conservation of natural resources" (16 USC 824a). To achieve this objective the Commission is directed to divide the country into regional coordination districts, after consultation with state commissions. The Commission's initial effort to use this authority was the publication of guidelines for voluntary regional interconnections in the 1964 *National Power Survey*. Implementation was left entirely to industry.

Pressured by public reaction to power failures, particularly the Northeast blackout of 1965, utilities began forming regional councils for the purpose of improving regional reliability. The reliability councils so formed are voluntary in nature and have no ultimate decision making authority in the area of planning. At present there are nine regional councils: East Central Area Reliability Coordination Agreement (ECAR), covering most of the Ohio Valley; Electric Reliability Council of Texas (ERCOT), a Texas intrastate council; Mid Atlantic Area Coordination Group (MACC); Mid America Interpool Network (MAIN), covering Illinois, parts of Missouri, Wisconsin, and Michigan; Mid Continent Area Reliability Coordination Agreement (MARCA), covering a large portion of the North Central states; Northeast Power Coordinating Council (NPCC); Southeastern Electric Reliability Council (SERC); Southwest Power Pool Coordination Agreement (SPP), covering the South Central states exclusive of Texas; and Western Systems Coordinating Council (WSCC), covering the entire western half of the country.

Each of the regional councils is a member of the National Electric Reliability Council (NERC) which was formed in 1968 to increase the reliability of bulk power supply. NERC encourages interregional arrangements through the exchange of information and review of regional and interregional activities. Federal Power Commission and state commission representatives have the right of nonvoting participation in the regional councils and in NERC. The FPC also receives projected load growth and coordination of bulk power supply information in annual reports from the councils. The councils agree to coordinate and submit for review their plans for new bulk power facilities. The agreements are intended to insure that individual regional plans do not adversely affect those of other systems or of the interconnected regional network. Since the councils cannot compel action on the part of any of their members it is difficult to gauge their actual impact on utility decision making. At a minimum, they would appear to force utilities into thinking in terms of area reliability and future joint development.

In March 1973 the Commission revised the annual filing requirement of the Councils to require both 10- and 20-year load and capacity data projections; data on seasonal peak loads and fuel requirements; itemization of existing capacity resources in the region and new capacity resources committed or projected for each 10 years; reports on primary fuels; capability for alternative fuel use; environmental control plans for steam plants projected or under construction; projections for transmission line routes, and percentages of capacity projected for hydroelectric, nuclear, or fossil-fueled plants.

The Advantages of Pooling—A Digression

Even before the establishment of the voluntary regional councils, utilities began forming regional planning and pooling arrangements. The practical stimulus to joint planning was the capital market. In view of efficient unit sizes and required capital commitments, some form of joint participation appeared advantageous for all but the largest systems.

Regional power pooling allows joint planning and operation of facilities, makes the exchange of economy energy easier, prevents construction of unnecessary facilities by isolated systems and increases reliability. Present pooling agreements, while representing a vast improvement over isolated utility operations, are far from ideal.

As defined by the Federal Power Commission's 1970 National Power Survey (I-17-2):

> The term "formal power pool" as used here means two or more electric systems which coordinate the planning and/or operation of their bulk power facilities for the purpose of achieving greater economy and reliability in accordance with a contractual agreement that establishes each member's responsibilities. Individual members usually are able to obtain the economies and other advantages available to much larger systems while retaining their separate corporate identities.

So considered, a "pool" can take many forms, from a bilateral agreement between two utilities to support one another with emergency backup, to the joint construction efforts which marked the development of nuclear generation capacity in New England or of the extra high voltage transmission tie between utilities in the Pacific Northwest and California. Pooling also can include a sophisticated multilateral pact which seeks to insure that at any specified level of demand, consumers in an integrated region will be served by the most efficient equipment then available, whether or not it is owned by the utility whose customers have generated the load.

The pools are dominated by the larger utility systems, prejudicing their smaller associates and raising antitrust questions. Moreover, there is no opportunity for public input at the initial decision making stages. But these deficiencies need not be typical of industry performance.

For example, as a result of transmission ties, pooling offers distinct economies to participating systems and environmental savings to society generally. Because of time-of-day load diversities (and the noncoincidental occurrence of the peaks of participating systems) it is possible to reduce the total capacity requirement that otherwise would apply were each system charged with fully meeting its needs. By consolidating the available capacity of several utilities, it is possible to significantly reduce the amount of reserve capacity required. As described by the FPC 1970 National Power Survey, (I-17-4):

> A power pool must have sufficient generation capacity to meet the combined pool load plus reserve to cover equipment outages, frequency regulation, load swings, errors in forecasting loads, and slippage in planning and construction schedules. The various pools make specific provision for sharing among the pool participants the burden of providing this reserve margin. There are, in general, two different methods of accomplishing this objective. Under one, each member is required to maintain a specified minimum capacity reserve, usually stated in percent of peak load. Under the other, existing installed generating capacity is shared on an equalized reserve basis. That is, rather than each member's being responsible for maintaining some minimum amount of reserve, the reserve capacity of the pool is shared proportionally among the members. Reserve responsibility is satisfied by capacity transactions so that members with excess capacity resources are compensated by members having capacity deficiencies.

In addition to the operational cost savings that can be realized through broad-based economy dispatch. the reduction of peak capacity and reserve requirements, and the realization of economies of scale (where they still exist as in the case of extra high voltage transmission facilities), pooling facilitates financing. With capacity costs increasing and utility interest coverage ratios approaching minimum trust indenture specifications, it will be difficult for even the larger system to finance unilaterally the massive capacity installations projected for the next two decades. If smaller utilities are denied access to (that is, denied the right to share ownership of) relatively more efficient capacity, they will fail to add to their rate bases, and will consequently be put at a disadvantage in the equity capital market. Financing may then become prohibitive and their viability as bulk power suppliers will be seriously threatened.

Pooling also offers the social advantage of maximizing environmental efficiencies. It is not economically or environmentally efficient to pollute every river or lake a little or contaminate every air basin, especially since capacity concentrations facilitate cleanup efforts. Once water or air quality begins to deteriorate it is time to minimize treatment cost through scale economies at a single site, and preserve the environmental quality of selected locations and ecosystems.

Duplication of generation or transmission facilities results in a misallocation of resources. Maximum use of each site, multiple use of existing transmission rights-of-way, and their conversion into interutility transmission corridors are possible. Moreover, the locations suitable for large nuclear or fossil-fired generating stations are limited. Inevitably there will be a movement in the direction of generating farms (or clusters of units and plants on a single site) in an attempt to localize the externalities associated with the production of electricity (particularly after underground extra high voltage transmission technology is perfected and becomes economically feasible).

An additional concern is occasioned by the reliance upon nuclear generating plants. Is there a sufficient cadre of technologists to staff every separate utility that has or will enter the field of nuclear generation? What would it cost to create such a cadre? As the public becomes more aware of the potential for hazard associated with nuclear generation, attention will be focused on the quality of nuclear managers. Joint operation of nuclear facilities (which has been the practice in New England) minimizes the need for technical expertise.

Pooling introduces diversity of management philosophy into the corporate decision making process.[ff] However, the benefits of management diversity will be achieved only to the extent that the pool planning process is open to the managements of public and private, small and large utilities, and to the views of the public as well. It would appear that pooling permits the realization of the economic and social cost minimizing options open to the largest of utility systems while extending those benefits to a segment of the industry to which they otherwise would be denied.[gg]

What the FPC Can Do

Pooling agreements are tariffs, and as such they must be filed with the Federal Power Commission, which has discretionary authority under its rate provisions to examine the propriety of the details and make appropriate modifications.

[ff]The testimony of Louis Roddis, Jr., President of Consolidated Edison, in the American Electric Power-Columbus and Southern merger proceeding before the Securities and Exchange Commission (SEC Adm. File No. 3-1476), is instructive on this point. It was his judgment that the diversity of management philosophy available to the pool as it discharges its planning functions leads to decisions being "thought through in greater depth than . . . if one company had been doing it" (Tr. 12451). The FPC's Bureau of Power agrees (A Study of the Electric Power Situation in New England, *1970-1990* (June 1971), p. 15):

> Differing views as to how to achieve the most reliable and economic bulk power supply system should precipitate consideration of reasonable alternatives which might be overlooked by a central autonomous agency. No organizational structure by itself, can provide assurance that the best decisions will always be made but the broader the base upon which decisions are couched, the better should be their quality.

[gg]In the American Electric Power-Columbus and Southern merger proceeding, Mr. Roddis was asked (Tr. 12454):

Q. Can you think of any kind or kinds of benefits or savings, exclusive of administrative savings, that a holding company under single management could attain that a power pool or other form of joint and cooperative efforts could not attain?

A. Given the same people and the same degree of effort, no.

The rate standard of the Federal Power Act provides (Section 205(b), 16 USC 824d(b)):

> No public utility shall, with respect to any transmission or sale subject to the jurisdiction of the Commission, (1) make or grant any undue preference or advantage to any person or subject any person to any undue prejudice or disadvantage, or (2) maintain any unreasonable difference in rates, charges, service, facilities, or in any other respect, either as between localities or as between classes of service.

This is a significant source of authority that demands that the Federal Power Commission test the provisions of a pooling agreement against the statutory proscriptions. Any differential treatment among systems is per se unreasonable and unduly preferential unless the proponents can prove otherwise.

Pooling among systems of different size can be advantageous to all systems, including the larger ones. In most instances there should be considerable room to negotiate differences. Moreover, with the assistance of a state commission (which alone can trigger jurisdiction under Section 207 of the Federal Power Act (16 USC 824f)), the Federal Power Commission, if it

> shall find that any interstate service of any public utility is inadequate or insufficient . . . shall determine the proper, adequate, or sufficient service to be furnished, and shall fix the same by its order, rule, or regulation. . . . [The only explicit limitations are that the Commission is without] authority to compel the enlargement of generating facilities for such purpose, and without authority to compel the public utility to sell or exchange energy when to do so would impair its ability to render adequate service to its customers.

Sections 202(b) and 202(c) explicitly authorize the Commission to order the enlargement of transmission facilities. The Commission can, in times of emergency and acting either on its own motion or upon application by any interested person, direct

> temporary connections of facilities and such generation, delivery, interchange, or transmission of electric energy as in its judgment will best meet the emergency and serve the public interest. . . . [Emergency is defined to include] a sudden increase in the demand for electricity, or a shortage of electric energy or of facilities for the generation or transmission of electric energy, or of fuel or water for generating facilities or other causes. . . .

The Commission has historically approached Section 202 timidly. Yet the courts have been willing to accept the Commission's exercise of expert judgment if they are convinced that the Commission has considered all relevant factors in the decisionmaking process.[hh] In view of the emergency created by environmental siting constraints, by financing limitations, and by the threatened disappearance of smaller systems, a reappraisal of the potential offered by Section 202 is in order.

The Federal Power Commission, when discharging its regulatory functions, may not ignore the national policy implicit in the antitrust laws.[ii] Those laws hold that those in a monopoly position may not refuse to deal, or deny access to essential facilities, or allocate territories, or otherwise act to use a position of economic dominance unfairly, to preclude competition.[jj]

Two recent decisions of the Supreme Court warrant particular consideration. *Otter Tail Power Co. v. United States,*410 U.S. 366, 41 L.W. 4293 (February 22, 1973) and *Gulf States Utilities v. FPC,*411 U.S. 747, 41 L.W. 4637 (May 14, 1973). In *Otter Tail* the Court held that a private company's refusal to "wheel" or sell power to municipals violated the antitrust laws. "Wheeling" involves the use of a third party's transmission facilities to effect the delivery of power from a producer to a distributor. In *Gulf States* the Court overturned the Commission's refusal to consider antitrust implications.

The Court made it plain that anticompetitive factors were relevant to the discharge of all the Commission's regulatory responsibilities under Part II of the Federal Power Act (including its rate authority, a point conceded by the FPC). The Commission is under an explicit mandate to consider anticompetitive factors in discharging its Part I licensing functions (16 USC 803(h)). Last, the

The Commission could exercise licensing and recapture leverage to encourage regional planning. When a hydroelectric license issued by the Federal Power Commission expires and it is considering whether to issue a new license to the original licensee, it is appropriate to consider its performance as a utility neighbor. Did it facilitate or block efficient regional planning? Hydroelectric plants are valuable peaking assets and will become increasingly so as the availability of sites declines. The Federal Power Commission should use its broad conditioning authority to insure that a licensee acts as a good utility "citizen." Of course no less should be required of a new licensee.

[hh]Compare *Otter Tail Power Co. v. FPC*, 429 F.2d 232 (CA 8, 1970) certiorari denied 401 U.S. 947 and *Florida Power Corp. v. FPC*, 425 F.2d 1196 (CA 5, 1970) reversed on other grounds, 403 U.S. 910.

[ii]See *United States v. El Paso Natural Gas Co.*, 376 U.S. 651 (1964) and *Northern Natural Gas Co. v. FPC*, 399 F.2d 953 (CADC, 1968).

[jj]See *Eastman Kodak Co. v. Southern Photo Materials Co.* 372 U.S. 359 (1927); *Associated Press v. United States*, 326 U.S. 1 (1945); *United States v. Topco Associates*, 405 U.S. 546 (1972); and *United States v. Aluminum Company of America*, 148 F.2d 416 (CA 2, 1945).

A recent order of the Iowa State Commerce Commission deserves mention. Concerned that the absence of adequate interutility interconnections was causing utilities to rely on capacity that depended on scarce fuels, it stated on May 18, 1973 (Order No. 73-01):

> It shall be the policy of this Commission to encourage the electric utilities operating within the State of Iowa to voluntarily establish and maintain interconnections of their electric transmission facilities whenever and wherever practical and feasible, and to enter into agreements for the sale and purchase of electric power and energy for the purposes of conserving liquid and gaseous hydrocarbon fuels, and achieving economies in the costs of generation of electrical energy ultimately purchased by consumers within the State of Iowa. In the event voluntary interconnections of facilities and agreements for the sale and purchase of electric power and energy are not forthcoming, the Commission shall utilize all of the resources at its command to obtain orders under the Federal Power Act directing the establishment of physical connections of facilities and the sale and purchase of electric power and energy to achieve the above-stated purposes.

The apparent intention of the order was to invoke the authority of the Federal Power Commission under Section 207 of the Federal Power Act. Each Iowa utility is "to report to the Commission, within 60 days of the issuance of [the] statement, the results of their efforts to achieve voluntary interconnections and sales and purchase agreements." Other state commissions might follow this example by examining the adequacy of existing interconnections and, where deficient, prodding the Federal Power Commission to use its authority, which has been dormant.

In summary, there exists substantial leverage and authority by which the Federal Power Commission could promote meaningful and open regional planning, coordination, and integration. At a minimum the Commission should insist that every pooling agreement extend its benefits to any utility in the region which desires to participate on an equitable basis in economy dispatch and joint ownership arrangements. The Commission may legitimately investigate refusals to sell, to wheel, or to interconnect where such arrangements would be in the public interest.

SECURITIES AND EXCHANGE COMMISSION

The Securities and Exchange Commission has regulatory responsibilities over the electric utility industry as a consequence of the 1933 Securities and Exchange Commission Act and the 1935 Public Utility Holding Company Act. Under the latter the Commission is concerned with the financing (both debt and equity capital) of holding companies (both electric and gas) and with their acquisition of other entities (15 USC 79 et seq.). The 1935 Act authorizes the SEC to regulate utility holding companies in order to prevent or eliminate large, complex systems that could circumvent regulation, concentrate political power, and create economically unstable corporate structures.

Electric utilities were once local firms regulated by municipalities. But technology developed and demand increased. Economies of scale were achieved through the construction of larger, more efficient generating plants. The plants were often located outside of municipal boundaries, complicating effective local regulation. State regulatory commissions were therefore created. Rapid technological advances and the increasing importance of electricity in the national economy increased the attractiveness of investment in electric utilities. It became apparent that through the holding company device a relatively small percentage of stock ownership could result in the control of an operating utility. Moreover, multistate holding companies were able to avoid the rigors of state commission regulation. Financial abuses were prevalent.[kk]

By the 1920s utility holding company systems had gained such a dominant status in the industry that a Senate-directed Federal Trade Commission investigation was begun. In 1934 the President appointed a National Power Policy Committee on Public Utility Holding Companies. Both efforts confirmed the need for corrective legislation.

That legislation, the Public Utility Holding Company Act, placed holding companies under the jurisdiction of the Securities and Exchange Commission. Holding companies are defined as those companies which directly or indirectly control 10 percent or more of the oustanding voting securities of a public utility (or of a holding company) or which, in the judgment of the SEC, can exercise a sufficient influence over such an entity as to make regulation appropriate. Unless exempted by the Commission, each holding company must file a registration statement and its acquisitions are subject to prior approval.

By SEC order each registered holding company and subsidiary must limit its operations to a "single integrated public-utility system, and to such other businesses as are reasonably incidental, or economically necessary or appropriate to the operations of such integrated public utility system" (Section 11, 15 USC 79K). The Commission may, however, permit a registered holding company to continue to control one or more additional integrated systems if each of the following three conditions is met: (1) those systems would lose "substantial economies" if forced to operate independently; (2) all additional systems are in one state or in adjoining states or a contiguous foreign country; and (3) the continued combination of such systems would not impair the advantages of localized management, efficient operation, or the effectiveness of regulation.

[kk]See Thompson, *Confessions of a Power Trust* (1932) and *Integration of Public Utility Holding Companies*, Michigan Legal Studies, 1954.

Under the last proviso the Commission may also permit retention of an interest in any other business as reasonably incidental or economically necessary to the operations of one or more integrated public utility systems. In order to qualify it must be shown that such retention is either necessary or appropriate in the public interest or for protection of investors or consumers, and is not detrimental to the functioning of the system. The definition of "integration" has been determined on a case by case basis. The primary requisite has been the demonstration of economic feasibility. Mere physical integration, however, can be insufficient. Operational coordination is required.

The Commission has held that electric and gas systems do not qualify as integrated systems; this view was sustained by a Court of Appeals.[ll] But it is possible for a utility to retain a gas or electric business under the additional operations proviso. The acquisition of securities or utility assets of a public utility by a holding company is permitted only when the acquisition encourages the creation of an integrated system (Section 10, 15 USC 79j). The acquisition will not be approved if it is found that it will result in a concentration of control of public utility companies that will be detrimental to the public interest or the interest of investors or consumers.

Throughout the 1950s the SEC simplified holding company systems by requiring the divestiture of nonintegrated parts of a system. But the events of the 1960s and 1970s predisposed the Commission to approve existing holding companies' requests to acquire additional operating properties. The justification for expanding the systems was increased economy and efficiency. In the 1960s the number of merger proposals brought before the SEC doubled that of the past decade.[mm] In reviewing acquisition requests the Commission is obliged to give full consideration to national antitrust policies.[nn]

One further provision of the Holding Company Act should be noted, particularly since future structural options are considered below. Under Section 30 (15 USC 79z-4):

> The Commission is authorized and directed to make studies and investigations of public utility companies, the territories served or which can be served by public utility companies and the manner in which the same are or can be served, to determine the *sizes, types* and *locations* of public utility companies which do or can operate most economically and efficiently in the public interest, in the interest of investors and consumers, and in furtherance of a wider and more economical use of gas and electric energy; upon the basis

---

[ll]See *Philadelphia Company v. S.E.C.*, 177 F.2d 720 (D.C. Circuit, 1949).

[mm]See Hearings before the Senate Subcommittee on Antitrust and Monopoly, 91st Cong., 2nd Sess. (1970), p. 563.

[nn]See *Municipal Electric Association of Massachusetts v. SEC*, 413 F.2d 1052 (District of Columbia Circuit, 1969).

of such investigations and studies the Commission shall make public from time to time the recommendations as to the type and size of geographically and economically integrated public utility systems, which, having regard for the nature and character of the locality served, can best promote and harmonize the interests of the public, the investor and the consumer. . . . (Emphasis added.)

Under the 1933 Securities and Exchange Commission Act the Commission's jurisdiction extends to all public utilities whether or not they are part of holding company systems. The Act requires, as a condition to the issuance of any security (debt or equity), registration of the security and its associated prospectus with the Commission. The Commission may require information (15 USC 77(g) and (j)) necessary for the protection of the public and of investors.[oo] In fact, the SEC has recently amended its registration forms to require disclosure of the effects of environmental regulatory statutes (SEC Release 20549) and factual descriptions of environmentally related administrative or judicial proceedings affecting the business of the registrant.

The SEC's ability to influence rate design under the Public Utility Holding Company Act of 1935 is remote at best. But under the Securities and Exchange Commission Act of 1933, the Commission could play a significant though indirect role in rate design. As noted the 1933 Act requires the registration of debt and equity securities and the filing of prospectuses. The object of each requirement is protection of the public generally and of the investing public in particular. If a utility is experiencing an erosion of its earnings as a consequence of the failure of tail block rates to recover their full cost of service, investors should be alerted. Their response might force the company to reconsider its unrealistic rate structures.

If new capacity is constructed to supply increased tail block sales that are not fully remunerative, a further attrition of earnings will result; investors will be subject to the decisions of utility commissions when rate relief is sought. (Repetitive rate filings will undoubtedly force state commissions to examine rate policies to determine whether or not they are contributing to earnings erosion.) If relief is not granted following the expansion of plant, investors would be prejudiced significantly; if granted, it will mean that utilities and their investors will be protected from the losses resulting from inefficient growth that would not be tolerated in a free (nonregulated) market situation.

The Commission must be concerned with the ability of a utility's financial structure to support expansion. If a utility is growing in an inefficient manner it could precipitate a cash flow problem and justify an SEC decision to refuse authorization of expansion. Whenever confronted with a registration statement or prospectus the Commission should require detailed discussion of

[oo]See *Wilko v. Swan*, 346 U.S. 427 (1953); *Oklahoma-Texas Trust v. SEC*, 100 F.2d 888 (1939).

the earnings attrition problem, notwithstanding the fact that such a discussion may influence the cost of capital. To the extent that the holding company's request (under the 1935 Act) to expand its capital may be attributed to the expansion of the company's generating capacity, the Commission should demand evidence that plant expansion will not lead to the further erosion of earnings.

ATOMIC ENERGY COMMISSION

Unlike the Federal Power Commission, which was established to regulate an existing generation technology, the Atomic Energy Commission was created to foster and promote a fledgling domestic nuclear electric generating industry. This objective, coupled with the fact that atomic energy involves highly dangerous materials useful for military purposes, shaped the framework for regulating the industry in some interesting and unusual ways. Initially, absolute control over nuclear materials was vested in the AEC, which was designated as keeper of the atom. As a result, no person could acquire, possess, or transfer any nuclear materials or any means of producing or using such materials without a license from the Commission (42 USC 2073, 2091, 2131).

With the development of nuclear technology and expertise the absolute nature of AEC control has begun to loosen to the point where restricted private ownership of nuclear materials is now permissible. Only the AEC may set standards for the discharge of effluents from nuclear power plants, however.[pp]

The basic legislation governing atomic energy is the Atomic Energy Act of 1954 (41 USC 2011). The Act states a policy of directing atomic energy development for peaceful purposes subject to "paramount" defense objectives. It requires that the AEC exercise a dual role as both promoter and regulator of nuclear power, a marriage of responsibilities that many citizen groups consider a basic conflict of interest, which they have challenged in the courts.[qq] The purposes of the Act include, "the fostering of research, dissemination of information . . . and encouraging participation in the development of atomic energy. . . ."

An applicant for a nuclear power plant license must obtain both a construction permit and an operating license. The construction permit application must indicate the type of reactor to be built, its chief safety characteristics and the features of the proposed site. A showing of final design specifications is not required at this stage. In addition, the applicant is required to submit an environmental report, which serves as the basis for the impact

---

[pp]See *Northern States Power Company v. State of Minnesota*, 447 F.2d 1143 (8th Circuit, 1971).

[qq]See *Conservation Society of Southern Vermont, et al. v. AEC* (Civil Action No. 19-72, District of Columbia).

statement which the AEC itself must prepare under NEPA. The application is reviewed and evaluated by the Division of Reactor Licensing. The Division of Reactor Safety then prepares a preliminary safety analysis report (PSAR), which includes an evaluation of plant design, the site, fuel handling and storage, radioactive waste disposal, the potential for accidents, the consequences to be expected from releases of radioactive materials into the environment, and the technical competence of the applicant.

Construction permit applications are also reviewed by the Advisory Committee on Reactor Safeguards (ACRS) which must determine whether a permit can be granted "without undue risk to the public." No environmental matters, except as they relate to public health and safety, are considered by the ACRS. Its recommendations, while not binding, are usually persuasive with the regulatory staff. The applicant's environmental report is reviewed by a special environmental staff within the regulatory division which also prepares the Commission's draft environmental impact statement.

All the foregoing reviews are followed by a mandatory public hearing before an "Atomic Safety and Licensing Board." Such hearing is required by NEPA in order to consider all relevant environmental factors. To find in favor of the license applicant the Board must determine that there is "reasonable assurance that the . . . proposed facility can be constructed and operated at the proposed location without undue risk to the health and safety of the public" (10 CFR 2.104(b) (1) (d)). Its decision can be challenged before the Atomic Safety and Licensing Appeals Board and, ultimately, in a Federal Appeals Court.

Once a permit has been issued, construction may begin. When the plant nears completion the utility will apply for an operating license, at which time the review process will begin again. However, a public hearing is not mandatory unless the grant of a license is contested. Shortly after requesting an operating license, a utility generally will file a request for authorization to conduct necessary tests to bring the plant to operational status, including fuel loading and the verification of facility performance.

The size, nature, and cost of large nuclear generating facilities make access to the resulting bulk power supply crucial to small systems in the region. Therefore, as a result of a 1970 amendment to its legislation, the AEC is now required to inform the Department of Justice of all construction permit applications. Within 180 days of such notification the AEC may be required to hold a special hearing on antitrust issues—if the Attorney General indicates that granting the permit could precipitate antitrust problems.

Two initiatives have been undertaken by the AEC in an effort to expedite the licensing process: standardization and generic proceedings. Under the former the Commission would license a manufacturer's standardized reactor design. Individual power plant hearings (the present construction permit stage) thereafter would be limited to site related issues. Much of the impetus for standardization comes from the work being done on the development of offshore nuclear power plants. Standardization of offshore reactor designs would expedite individual construction permit hearings.

Generic hearings would be used to resolve recurring substantive issues (such as the "as low as practicable" standard and the acceptability of the controversial emergency core cooling system) and thereby remove them from individual licensing proceedings. Presumably by focusing on a discrete major issue that is quite complex in nature the participation of interested groups would be made easier, and the factors relevant to the decisionmaking process would be developed more fully.

In addition to the requirements imposed by NEPA, the Commission's siting regulations consider, among other factors, population density and seismology to assure that the radiological effects of both normal and unanticipated plant operations will be minimized. Licensees are obliged to limit radiological releases into areas beyond their exclusive control to levels that are "as low as practicable," a standard which received some numerical definition in June 1971 when the Commission published proposed operating guidelines for light water cooled reactors (see Appendix I to 10 CFR).

The proposed criteria are intended to limit the radiation exposure to any organ of an individual at the site boundary to 5 millirems from liquid effluents. In terms of the general population, exposure is not to exceed an average dose of 1.7 millirems. A plant operator is permitted to exceed these limits if the excessive releases are short term and will not result in annual dose exposure to any organ of an individual in excess of 5 millirems for liquid or gaseous effluents. Although the numerical "as low as practicable" limits have not as yet been determined finally by the Commission, all plants currently being licensed are subject to those limitations. This requirement has presented problems for operators of boiling water reactors but not for those of pressurized water reactors.

Recognizing that the failure to provide liability protection could constitute a major obstacle to private development of the nuclear industry,[rr] Congress enacted the Price-Anderson Act (42 USC 2210), which limits the liability of a utility and its equipment suppliers, in the event of a nuclear power plant catastrophe, to 560 million dollars.

Under the National Environmental Policy Act, the AEC must consider reasonable alternatives to a nuclear project when an application for such a plant is under consideration. If the demand for electricity is price elastic, an alternative to additional capacity as proposed by a utility would be rate schedule revisions.

Although the AEC recognizes that electric consumption is price

---

[rr]The AEC's Brookhaven Report, better known as "Wash-740," calculated the destruction that would be caused by a nuclear accident at over 30,000 dead and 7 billion dollars in property damage.

elastic, it does not require discussion of rate design alternatives.[ss] This prejudices any later statewide rate case, because once the AEC authorizes new capacity (which often precedes the contemplated on-line service date by more than five years) the economic thrust will favor the use of rates designed to stimulate use. If excess capacity is authorized, rates will be set to use such capacity to achieve lower unit costs; this in turn will cause an increase in demand, and thus an invidious growth circle is perpetuated.[tt]

To avoid these difficulties the question of "need" (with its rate component) should be analyzed in advance of construction authorizations. Its resolution may fall outside the competence of the AEC. The need question may either be referred to the FPC for analysis and recommendation or referred to an FPC-state joint board. Since the state commission will confront the rate implications of any AEC determination directly, the latter would appear to be the preferable alternative. In view of the strong evidence that demand is sensitive to price, the AEC should question extrapolated demand projections predicated on declining block rates. At a minimum, forcing the utilities to explain rate practices in licensing cases would at least reemphasize the impact of price on consumption practices.[uu]

[ss]Draft Guide for the Preparation of Environmental Impact Statements.

[tt]The AEC recently had directed the consideration of conservation options in a licensing proceeding. See In the Matter of Niagara Mohawk Power Corporation, Docket No. 50-410, order issued November 7, 1973.

[uu]It should be noted that what has been said with respect to nuclear power plant licenses applies equally to hydroelectric license applications filed with the FPC. See *Scenic Hudson Preservation Conference v. FPC*, 354 F.2d 608 (CA 2, 1965), certiorari denied 384 U.S. 941 and *Udall v. FPC*, 387 U.S. 428 (1967)) and thermal plants that require permits under the Federal Water Pollution Control Act.

Chapter Five

Reorganizing Regulation

In Chapter Four we suggested ways in which the regulation of the electric power industry could be improved within the existing legal framework. The FPC-state joint board mechanism provided for in the Federal Power Act could greatly facilitate regional planning and rate regulation. But the joint board doesn't represent the optimal regulatory response—for example, the board would not eliminate the vagaries of federal and state legislative requirements. Licensing jurisdiction would remain severed from rate regulation, nuclear licensing would remain outside the reach of the board, and the siting of thermal plants would remain subject to the influence of varying state requirements.

Because the joint board would not require an abdication of state or federal sovereignty, it would only supplement existing regulatory procedures. Its effectiveness then would depend upon the willingness of each participant to subordinate individual prerogatives to regional objectives. The participants could not be forced to accept the decisions of the board. Consequently the board does not constitute a regulatory authority capable of implementing regional planning on a long term basis. In addition, the development of a national extra or ultra high voltage transmission grid would precipitate interregional problems that the board would not have the authority to resolve.

QUESTIONS AND SUGGESTIONS

In this chapter and in Chapter Six we turn to structural questions and offer suggestions for industry and regulatory realignments. It should be understood that the previous chapters represent a synthesis of generally accepted facts and of principles for efficient pricing of electricity. We expect that questions which have arisen thus far in the minds of readers are most likely to pertain to the specific relevance of particular items or to the pace of implementation of the principles. Hereafter, our purpose is to question the desirability of maintaining the existing structure of the electric power industry and its regulatory framework. Inevitably, institutional questions are less traceable than the comparatively straightforward microeconomic propositions that concerned us earlier.

While the following chapters concerning the industrial regulatory infrastructure of the electric power sector are not intended merely to be provocative, we believe it is clear that at least some part of the broad range problems that flow from increased electric power demand and supply are neither temporary nor solely financial. The regulated power sector is a creature of evolution, and we should not assume that its structure at one point will be an enduring model forever.

Regulatory Modeling

In approaching regulatory modeling it is important to begin with an understanding of objectives one hopes to realize. Stated most succinctly, it is to minimize private and social costs and to properly allocate responsibility for each. But it is not enough to talk in terms of cost minimization for a reduction in private costs to a firm may well increase the level of social costs. There is a definite tradeoff and need for a balancing apparatus. The marketplace might serve as the appropriate arbiter were only private costs involved. It cannot be relied upon to minimize externalities, however. Regulation must discharge this role, bring about overall balancing, and distribute revenue responsibilities among users with unequal bargaining strength.

It may seem ironic that our frustration with existing regulation has prompted a call for even more comprehensive controls. Present failures rest not with the logic of regulation, but with the chaotic and fragmented fashion in which it is now imposed. We do not view the relevant choice to be between regulation and deregulation. The issue becomes the perfection of regulation.

The recommendation we offer would result in the creation of comprehensive regional regulatory mechanisms. It would be possible to justify a regional approach by tracing the industry's development alone. When the industry first began with the construction of individual central station plants, it was local in character, as were its problems (e.g., retail rates, tax base, zoning). It was appropriate for the developing regulatory mechanism to be patterned after the emerging industry structure.

Around the turn of the century, regulation took on a statewide character responding to the emerging intercity status of the industry. In 1935 Congress recognized the interstate character of the industry and the resulting inability of any state regulatory body to provide appropriation supervision. Accordingly, the Federal Power Commission was given a regulatory role. Now the industrial unit is multistate in both its form and its implications. The industry itself has recognized the need to form regional relationships. Therefore, it is necessary to recognize the industry's historical transformation and to develop a regulatory mechanism that is capable of responding to industry as it now exists.

We favor the creation of regional regulatory commissions merging within each the greater portion of authority now exercised by national and state agencies. Our selection of a regional form was the logical result not only of our study of the evolution of the industrial unit to be regulated, but of the need to balance two somewhat competing tradeoffs: the desire for a capability to resolve major energy problems from a national perspective (particularly as we move toward a national transmission grid and seek to maximize the advantages of seasonal and time-of-day load variations) and the desire to bring the resolution of socioeconomic questions as close to the people affected as possible. The nation as a whole is too large a regulatory unit, and if used as such would inhibit the operation of democracy in the decision making process. At the same time, the typical state is simply too small a unit, given the present stage of technological development. With utilities planning their expansion activities on the basis of multistate pools, regulation cannot be effective if it can reach only a portion of the planning unit.

We recognize the fact that regional approaches to regulation do not enjoy the universal support of political scientists, many of whom argue that such mechanisms historically have failed to fulfill their expectations. We do not dispute the contention that ill-defined and vague efforts at regionalism panaceas have and will continue to fail. However, when the mandate has been precise, when the regional agency is forced to confront an existing phenomenon, regionalism has proven to be an effective planning and decision making mechanism.

The efforts of Bonneville in building a backbone transmission grid, and of the Tennessee Valley Authority in stimulating the economic development of a river valley, are very much in point and their successes are good precedents for the type of regional regulation we contemplate. Indeed, in many ways existing and emerging power pools are fixed realities very much like the existence of a river valley. We would expect each regional commission to more precisely define the goal of private and social cost minimization and the equitable allocation of burdens so that their achievement is most in harmony with any narrower regional objectives.

As will be apparent, the approach we suggest is not entirely without national and local inputs. We recognize the need for an interregional or national review mechanism and we would retain local regulation for what are purely intrastate problems. We suggest, in effect, a system of integrated regulation, in each case bestowing jurisdiction on the geographically smallest regulatory unit that is capable of discharging the particular responsibility.

Fragmentation

At present, jurisdictional fragmentation is a fact. The Federal Power Commission has siting authority over hydroelectric power plants and rate authority over interstate wholesale sales. The Atomic Energy Commission has siting authority over nuclear plants, but no rate authority. At least 26 state utility commissions have varying degrees of siting authority over steam electric plants and practically all state utility commissions have rate authority over intrastate retail sales. It is not the fact of fragmentation but the consequences of it that are objectionable.

Consider the effects of fragmented rate regulation. Assume that a utility sells energy to wholesale utility customers (who in turn resell to residential, commercial, and industrial users) and also distributes electricity directly to ultimate consumers. The utility's sales for resale are subject to the jurisdiction of the Federal Power Commission but its distribution activities are subject to state regulation. Assume further that a predominant share of the utility's capacity is coal-fired and it has been experiencing a steady, dramatic increase in fuel costs. The FPC, under its present policy, would permit the utility to include a full (100 percent) fuel cost adjustment clause in its wholesale rate schedules. However, in direct distribution to retail customers, the utility may either decline to include comparable tracking provisions, or may be rebuffed in its effort to do so by a state commission. The competitive implications are obvious. Wholesale sales to utility customers may be at a higher effective rate than direct sales to large industrial customers purchasing under declining block schedules. Wholesale customers are consequently denied the opportunity to compete for desirable high load factor industrial sales. Economic inefficiency prevails because prices are not based upon economic costs but upon regulatory differences.

Consider too the effect of licensing variations on power plant selection and siting decisions. A utility's decision to build a nuclear or a fossil fuel plant may be determined by differences in federal regulatory requirements. A utility's decision to locate a plant in one state rather than another may depend on differences in local regulatory requirements. Regulatory differences may be critical to a utility manager confronted with a lead time problem and responsibilities to a stockholder group; yet as far as the public interest is concerned they are extraneous considerations, which should not influence the corporate deliberative process.

Rate regulation is split between the Federal Power Commission and state utility commissions; licensing authority is split between the FPC, AEC, state commissions, and independent siting agencies. Inevitably, rate issues and siting questions are severed. Even where companion jurisdiction resides within a single agency, rate and siting questions have been considered independently because the utility company filing has traditionally defined the scope of the regulatory review. Consequently, siting and rate proceedings can be played against one another. Because of long construction and regulatory lead times, facility applications are filed several years before construction begins and are predicated on utility-supplied growth projections. As new capacity becomes available, rate schedules are designed to induce full use. The growth projections therefore become self-fulfilling prophecies. Rate design is virtually predetermined.

In view of the recent escalation in cost of new capacity, expansion of a utility system may well impose economic disadvantages on its customers. If regulators faced the implications of growth before they were committed to capacity additions, restructuring rate design might in some cases constitute a feasible alternative to expansion. Because growth dictates the need for capital attraction and consequently for rate relief, a comprehensive regulatory approach is essential. A single regulatory authority should be charged not only with the responsibility for site approval, but with consideration of the basic economic questions raised by expansion decisions.

Citizen Participation

While licensing proceedings have thus far served as the focal point for citizen participation, they are an inopportune time to confront the underlying issues of growth or environmental risks. Site selection is a process in which a utility implements a series of prior policy determinations. It is a means to a previously determined end. The end is the realization of a predetermined growth scenario, of a generation and transmission mix configuration, of contractual coordination, and of pooling objectives. Consequently utilities exhibit little patience with citizen intervenors who seek to raise rather basic demand or growth related issues during the licensing proceeding. In their view, and correctly so, the die has long since been cast. Rate policy too, whether it be the establishment of revenue levels or the formulation of rate design, has been used to accomplish predetermined objectives.

Obviously, there will be a need for more power plants regardless of the assumed growth scenario. Whether or not current environmental problems are solved, there will be social tradeoffs involving the nation's limited land, air, water, fuel, and transportation resources. But modifying existing regulatory procedures, addressed to the timely public disclosure of utility plans, the elimination of segmented applications, and making intercompany siting activities more effective falls short of addressing the underlying issues of who is to determine an area's rate of growth, or the extent to which it is to rely on nuclear as opposed to fossil fuel plants, or even the degree of reliability for which it is willing to pay.

If the regulatory process is to balance competing considerations in the public interest it must be exposed to all points of view—the conservationist's, the industrialist's, and the utility's. The current process makes it difficult to achieve this objective. The amount of resources required for an intervenor to confront a sophisticated and long planned utility proposal is staggering. The number of regulatory fronts makes the resource commitment cost prohibitive. Moreover, a layered regulatory process undermines even the limited authority of each regulatory participant. As the ball is passed to each succeeding agency there is pressure to keep it moving along, and not upset the thrust of previous determinations. The effect is to insulate the administrative process from public scrutiny. Since no one agency is truly responsible for the ultimate decision, no one agency can be held accountable.

State Solutions

Many of the deficiencies of the joint board approach also plague the numerous model state solutions that were proposed in the late 1960s–after the Northeast blackout of 1965 and the slightly less infamous mid Atlantic area outage of 1967.[a] Each of the proposals, although improving voluntary regional cooperation and requiring early disclosure of long range utility plans in varying degrees, relies primarily on a state certification process which may be subject to a federal override. State regulatory differences would remain part of the utility decision making process.

The major shortcoming of state solutions, as well as of the joint board approach, is that the problems to be solved are no longer intrastate problems. Extra high voltage transmission networks do not stop at political borders; feasible sites for large scale units are not available in all localities. States are under pressure to resist the location of facilities that are intended primarily for the benefit of consumers located in other states. The stability of an integrated regional network might be placed in jeopardy by local idiosyncracies. Moreover, the various schemes for state certification preserve the historical regulatory role, which is one of reaction, not initiation. While advance disclosure of long range plans is required and regional cooperation encouraged, the regulatory role is largely confined to the review of individual utility proposals.

Several states have responded to the power plant siting problem. Maryland expanded the authority of its Public Service Commission to include the certification of power plants and extra high voltage transmission lines. The Commission is obliged to prepare ten-year generation and transmission plans. An Environmental Trust, funded through a kilowatt hour surcharge, will support research and site acquisition activities. Utility proposals are now subject to an analysis similar to that required by the National Environmental Policy Act.

Rather than delegating primary regulatory authority to already existing commissions, New Hampshire created a new Site Evaluation Committee comprised of thirteen representatives from the state's planning and environmental control agencies. As with Maryland, long range siting plans are to be based on an analysis of utility filed ten-year projections. Both Maryland and New Hampshire merged responsibility for the certification of power plants and transmission lines.

In New York the existing public service commission, which exercises retail rate jurisdiction, was given responsibility for the certification of transmission lines alone. Jurisdiction over steam electric facilities was given to a board comprised of the Chairman of the Public Utility Commission, the Commissioners

---

[a]For an analysis of these early proposals see: *Electricity and the Environment, The Reform of Legal Institutions*, A Report of the Association of the Bar of the City of New York, West Publishing Company, 1972 (hereinafter referred to as the "N.Y. Bar Assn. Report"), Chap. VII; Journey, "Power Plant Siting–A Roadmap of the Problem," 48 Notre Dame Lawyer 273 (Dec., 1973).

of Environmental Conservation, Health and Commerce, and an ad hoc member appointed by the governor from the area affected by the proposal. In contrast to the Maryland siting legislation, the New York response represents a one-stop approach merging certification requirements to avoid overlap of state and local jurisdictions.

In Maryland localities can continue to exercise considerable regulatory control over the siting of utility facilities through zoning and building codes. This local regulation is in no way limited to Maryland. Unless a state has created a regulatory mechanism for one-stop certification with authority to override local regulation, utilities must abide by local zoning ordinances. Zoning regulations are implemented by local boards; generally variances or special exceptions can only be granted after public hearings. Some courts have overturned local zoning laws that bar the construction of generating plants. However, codes that are less absolute in effect and leave the ultimate determination to the discretion of an administrative authority are generally recognized as lawful exercises of local police power and must be complied with, even at the expense of relitigating issues previously considered at the state certification level.

The Association of the Bar of the City of New York has suggested that a national authority, through a constituent regional mechanism, determine long range regional capacity needs. Congress would have responsibility for setting policy regarding demand levels, and, where possible, generic proceedings would be used on both the state and federal level to resolve recurring issues (e.g., standard setting). Issues so resolved would be removed from individual certification proceedings. An effort would also be made to insure that each state will be required to accommodate within its boundaries an allocable share of the region's required generation and transmission facilities.

One difficulty with this innovative proposal is that while it properly focuses on regional needs for planning purposes, its reliance on utility initiatives and state certification processes leaves considerable room for the ultimate frustration of regional objectives. State commissions would continue to play a reactive role; utilities would be required to take the initiative by the filing of applications, and utilities could persist in the fragmentation of logically integrated proposals.

It is unclear what would happen if no utility chose to file an application to construct a portion of the state's allocated capacity requirement. Indeed, it is unclear how the state siting agency is to make certain that the utilities in its jurisdiction would be required to respond to the state's allocated capacity requirement. Even if each state met its allocated requirement, the licensing of facilities (particularly transmission facilities) might not follow the schedule most desirable from a regional standpoint.

The New York Bar Association's proposal assumes that developing a target growth rate requires the resolution of political questions. But so too does the question of whether an area will go nuclear or fossil, or will be willing to pay the price of a 20 percent as opposed to a 15 percent reserve margin. We argue that these issues should be resolved regionally, not at the national level. There is no reason why each region must be committed to the same generation mix or growth rate. The social tradeoffs involved might be weighted quite differently from region to region.

REGIONAL COMMISSIONS

If the objectives of long range planning are to be realized, if citizens are to be given a meaningful opportunity to address crucial issues, if the costs and benefits of production, distribution and consumption are to be equitably allocated, it is necessary that a public, accountable authority be given comprehensive regulatory control.

We favor the creation of regional electric power regulatory commissions, merging within each the siting and rate authority now exercised by federal and state agencies. The abdication of state responsibility over local rates assumes the continuation of the present industry structure. In the next chapter we recommend that distribution activities be severed from generation and transmission activities. We would then leave the responsibility for the regulation of retail rates with the states. Even with such a restructuring the regional commissions would initially exercise rate jurisdiction over generation and transmission entities in order to create an economic climate which permitted competition to determine the price of electricity at the wholesale level.

We recommend that the nation (with the exclusion of Alaska and Hawaii) be divided into regions, creating areas large enough (but no larger) to permit the realization of the technical advantages of cooperation such as economy dispatch of generation and the joint construction of facilities. The presently constituted regional reliability councils may offer appropriate points of departure but their existing configurations should not be accepted without detailed analysis. The FPC would conduct, over a one-year period, nationwide hearings focusing on the regional configurations. Six months later the FPC would announce its conclusions and following a brief opportunity for public comment, transmit its recommendations to the Congress.

The actual implementation of the regional scheme would depend upon Congressional action. We would merge within each regional commission all site certification responsibilities now exercised by the FPC, the AEC, and state power plant and transmission line licensing authorities; all federal and state jurisdiction over rates; and federal and state jurisdiction over industry structure (including the responsibilities of the Securities and Exchange Commission under the Public Utility Holding Company Act).

The regional authority would, within the limits hereafter described, totally preempt regulatory responsibilities now discharged by federal and state agencies. This is basic to the proposal. It is not our intention to graft another regulatory layer onto a system already too complex. Our objective is to simplify regulation, and accomplishing it depends on the willingness of each level of government to relinquish the limited authority it now exercises.

The regional commission would operate as a collegial commission composed of a chairman selected from the region by the President, with the advice and consent of the Senate, and an additional commissioner from each state (including the District of Columbia) represented in the region. A state might be included in more than one region. Each state would be free to establish its own procedures for the selection of its commissioner. If a state failed to complete its selection within a prescribed time the President would fill the vacancy for a limited period after which the state would again be free to act. Each commissioner, including the chairman, would sit for a prescribed term subject to reappointment and would be barred from accepting employment with or remuneration from a regulated entity for a period of two years following the completion of his term of office. The chairman of each regional agency would in addition serve as a member of a National Electric Power Coordinating Commission.

During the first two years of operation the regional commissions would not have licensing or rate setting authority; rather, certification and rate responsibilities would remain where they are now. This interim period would give the regional commission an opportunity to develop long range regional plans, before becoming bogged down with the need to resolve individual license and rate applications.[b] During this initial phase, each commission would undertake a comprehensive analysis of all existing pooling agreements between two or more utilities within its region. The Commissions would have full authority over contractual arrangements among utilities.

Congress decided, when it passed the 1935 Federal Power Act, that the nation could not afford an electric utility industry that failed to extend the benefits of cooperation to all utilities. The new legislation would encourage the development of a series of interutility operational arrangements designed to maximize regionwide consumer benefits. To the extent that existing arrangements inhibit the full realization of this objective (for example, by excluding smaller systems from economy dispatch procedures) a commission would be obliged to effect any appropriate modifications—including the voiding of existing contracts in favor of a new comprehensive pooling arrangement.

During the initial two-year period, each commission would develop a long term policy scenario for its region, focusing on all underlying generic issues such as the desired rate of growth, the allocations of capacity requirements

[b]The enactment of the National Environmental Policy Act found agencies unprepared to discharge the legislation's important, time consuming responsibilities. Consequently the early environmental impact statements were largely disappointing and caused agencies to hurriedly develop inadequate administrative procedures. It would be unfortunate if these difficulties were to be repeated by burdening the new regional entities with the need to resolve complex power supply issues before they had time to get their own houses in order.

among the various forms of available generation, the development of a long range regional transmission grid, and the promulgation of reliability criteria. Obviously this would result in the establishment of growth scenarios by nonelected officials. However, at the present time this essential decision is, for all practical purposes, made by industry. Thus, while our suggestion does not guarantee full "democratization," it does offer greater public accountability than now exists.

The plan thus developed would be updated and revised as appropriate upon application by any interested person or the commission acting *sua sponte* following a full public hearing which would be held at least once every five years. By approaching capacity additions on a regional basis it would be possible to avoid, or certainly to minimize, the "lumpiness" problem that results when utilities are required to add generation increments that far exceed their immediate needs. For example, a utility may need to augment its capacity by 100 megawatts but scale economies dictate the addition of a 500 megawatt unit. In this situation strong incentives exist to promote the full use of available new capacity at less than the long-run incremental cost of supplying that capacity and thus accelerate the need for further capacity additions. Regional integration will ameliorate the lumpiness problem by meeting the capacity requirements of a greater pool with greater flexibility.

While this initial regional planning effort is being discharged, each state would be required to certify to its respective regional commission a prescribed number of sites capable of accommodating generation facilities of varying types and sizes. Several sites, ranked from an environmental standpoint, should be selected for large base-load nuclear and fossil plants, and other sites designated for peaking installations. This would establish site selection as a matter of local concern and disposition, at least initially. It would be up to the states to develop their own mechanism for completing this selection. There would be a requirement, however, that the opportunity for public participation in the site identification process satisfy minimum guidelines established by the National Electric Power Coordination Commission.

In designating sites to a regional commission a state would certify that all local requirements (such as zoning) had been complied with and that each site was capable of accommodating the type of plant designated—detailing, for example, the availability of cooling water and ash disposal facilities. If a state should fail to identify its approved sites within the time period prescribed and within any subsequent periods prescribed for periodic updates (perhaps every three years), the regional commission would be free to preempt this authority and override local requirements that would otherwise apply. Adopting the advice of the New York Bar Association, site selection would be left to that level of government that has most at stake. If local government should fail to discharge its responsibilities it would abdicate its authority to act.

At the completion of its generic proceeding each regional commission would identify the size, type, and general location of facilities to be constructed over a prescribed period. Regional commissions would be required to allocate capacity among their constituent states roughly in proportion to each state's contribution to regionwide demand. The objective would be to have each state accept an equitable share of the externalities associated with the region's power supply. Some states may desire the location of new generation facilities as a means of stimulating employment and industrial activity; others may be better suited for the siting of specific facilities, such as mine mouth plants. Indeed, it might be preferable to locate generation farms in sparsely populated areas, while endeavoring to fully internalize all social costs.

But a state that is required to accept (or willingly accepts) the responsibility for more than its allocable share of generation should be compensated for the associated social costs by states relieved of that responsibility. This could be accomplished through an externality tax fund, which is discussed below.

Once the construction program is announced, any utility, or entity wishing to become a utility by the construction and operation of generating facilities, would be free to apply for a license for an indicated facility. All competing applications would be consolidated in one adversary proceeding, with interested members of the public afforded the right of full participation. The commission would be free to grant or deny any application and would enjoy broad conditioning authority. Thus a commission might authorize construction upon the condition that two or more applicants undertake the project jointly, or that a utility which could not itself construct the entire project be afforded an opportunity to participate in ownership. Among the public interest standards that would be applied in passing upon applications would be those explicit and implicit in the antitrust laws. In discharging its licensing authority, the regional commission would be obliged to secure a more competitive structure within the industry. Any utility would be free to reject an application approval that included conditions it found unacceptable.

At the comparative hearing the regional commission would attempt to certificate the proposal with the lowest private and social costs. There would be competition among potential bulk power suppliers for the right of entry. Each applicant would be required to document its financial and technical ability to perform and remain in business during the useful life of the project; to project capacity and energy costs that would result from certification of its proposal; and to estimate the externalities that would be involved.

It is conceivable that a regional commission would reject a lower cost proposal from an existing bulk power supplier in order to broaden the industry's competitive base through the entry of a new supplier whose private costs were somewhat higher. The regional commission would specify, through a certificate condition, the initial price at which the electricity to be produced at the project could be sold. Recognizing that costs could escalate before the project was brought on line, the commission would retain jurisdiction to readjust the price condition based upon a rate type of presentation.

Once a competitive structure evolved, and a sufficient number of wholesale suppliers assured the region of adequate wholesale price competition, the regional commissions would lose their rate jurisdiction. Efforts would have to be made to open up entry into the wholesale supply market. At present and for the most part, entry is limited to vertically integrated utility companies that both produce bulk power and distribute it at the retail level. The loss of rate jurisdiction over wholesale prices would not in any way diminish the regional commission's responsibility for regional planning and the regulation of entry of bulk power suppliers.

It is possible that no utility in the region would seek authorization to construct a facility identified in the long range plan prepared by the regional commission. In that event, if the commission felt the particular facility was necessary in the public interest, it could recommend to Congress that it be developed by a federal marketing agency. All federal marketing agencies and the Tennessee Valley Authority (indeed, all private or publicly owned utility systems) would be subject to the siting authority of the regional commissions. The federal marketing agencies would themselves be required to assist in the achievement of a competitive industry structure. Therefore they would be encouraged to invite new entrants to participate as joint builders and owners of generating projects. In this way a viable "small generation company" segment would be developed, a result not likely if small new entrants are required to shoulder the entire capital cost of new units built at the optimally efficient size.

Externality Tax Fund

Thus far, although it should be clear that the procedure recommended is of the one-stop variety, the responsibility for environmental standards has not been addressed. Standard setting might be delegated to the regional commissions by requiring that each authorized facility cause the minimum feasible adverse environmental affects. This would leave the commissions free to include the range of possible standards (thermal effect, particulate emission) in the ad hoc balancing process. Or standard setting might be left with the technical agencies which are now responsible for them. We favor the latter approach, believing that environmental standards that require due regard for the protection of human health should not be subject to barter in a power plant licensing proceeding. The procedure recommended is analogous to that established by the 1970 amendments to the Federal Water Pollution Control Act, which gave expert agencies the authority to set water quality standards to which licensing agencies would be bound.

Regional commissions would be responsible for the environmental impact of actions which they authorize. One of the objectives of regional rate regulation is to insure that the supplier recovers the full cost of service from its customers. Traditionally it has been assumed that if the supplier recoups all costs, the consumers will have in fact paid all appropriate costs.

But society pays a heavy price for the consequences of generation and transmission activities—the so-called externalities. To the extent that consumer prices recover only the utility's costs of supplying the power, the user is in fact being subsidized by society at large, or that portion of society which sustains the external costs. Where the subsidizing and user groups are identical the problem is somewhat less troublesome; but it is not avoided, since not everyone consumes at the same level or at the same time. However, such coincidence is unlikely when sites are located outside the area they serve.

The economic consequence of ignoring external costs is to price electricity at an artificially low level leading in turn to excessive consumption relative to other less socially costly goods and services. We do not suggest that electric consumption be subject to a surcharge, a penalty designed to discourage growth. We propose only that the cost to society of the pollution of water, land and air be assessed, and recovered. Obviously, the utility would be unjustly enriched were it permitted to retain the revenues resulting from the inclusion of such costs. The problem is to devise an appropriate recipient for the revenues associated with the costs suffered by society. The recently proposed sulfur emission tax supplies one answer. By assessing the tax against the utility the cost is internalized and allocated among the users as is any other cost of doing business.

A variation on the sulfur tax would be to set taxes in order to recoup the social costs or damages and pay them into the general treasury— either the federal treasury or that of the states—in proportion to the externalities that each is forced to shoulder. Or taxes might be set to create an incentive to meet pollution standards.

An extension of the tax idea that has some analogy within existing FPC authority offers a flexibility not available through taxing measures. Under the Federal Power Act 50 percent of annual charges assessed against licensees which make use of public land are paid into the Reclamation Fund. A fund receiving revenues associated with external costs could be used to compensate those made to bear those externalities. In a rate case two sets of costs would be fixed—those for which the utility is entitled to be reimbursed and those for which society as a whole (or the part damaged) is to be compensated. Rate schedules would be devised to recoup both sets of costs and the resulting revenues allocated appropriately between the fund and the utility. The regional externality fund would be an additional party to the rate proceeding, arguing for a sufficient measure of funds to compensate for the social costs of the utility operations. Only those costs not internalized by the utility would be subject to the externality fund mechanism.

Following the restructuring of industry and the creation of an independent and competitive bulk power supply segment, the regional commissions, although relinquishing rate jurisdiction, would continue to fix the payment to be made into the externality fund. They would do so as part of the certification process. After determining the externalities associated with each of the competing applications, the successful applicant would be required to pay into the fund an amount representing the anticipated social costs of its project. In this way, the costs are internalized and borne by the project's user beneficiaries.

It would be the responsibility of the fund to disburse its revenues in an effort to compensate society for the externality. Medical facilities or research efforts might be supported where the externalities have human health implications, or open space might be acquired to compensate for acreage lost to plant siting, or forest lands purchased and preserved where others are constructively taken by utility operations. It would be the function of the regional authority in expending its funds to endeavor to compensate society as precisely as possible for the amenity lost or the social costs incurred.

Critics will be quick to underscore the difficulty of determining the cost of the externalities. We acknowledge the difficulty. The sulfur tax represents an arbitrary response. In certain situations the problem will be less imponderable. For example, while it may be exceedingly difficult to cost out the human health implications of sulfur dioxide or particulate emissions, it should be relatively easy to put a price tag on lost physical assets (such as a mountain top dedicated to pump storage). If at the very least a rough cut is not attempted, this omission carries with it a decision to err on the side of underpricing electricity. Nonaction is not the equivalent of neutrality; it is markedly prejudicial. Failing to recognize external costs itself carries a marked degree of bias. External costs often are exacted from those members of society who are not responsible for the added capacity requirements.

National Electric Power
Coordinating Commission

The chairman of each regional commission would serve as a member of a national electric power coordinating commission. The jurisdiction of the national commission would be limited but critical. In addition to collecting coordination information and developing minimum public participation standards to govern the state site identification process, it would sit in the nature of an appellate body to review the action (and nonaction) of regional commissions alleged to be detrimental to utility operations and the public interest of another region. It is possible that actions required by one regional commission would impair the reliability of another region. These interregional difficulties should not, at least in the first instance, be resolved by the courts. The issues will be far too complex and require a detailed familiarity with the operational characteristics of multiple regions.

The structure we recommend may be compared to that of the

Federal Reserve System which, through regional banks, maintains a continual planning and regulatory relationship with banking institutions within each region, while retaining a national competence (the Federal Reserve Board) to meet problems of broader than regional scope. Hence, any interested person, including persons from other regions (as well as regional commissioners) concerned with the extraregional implications of a regional commission determination, would be free to invoke the jurisdiction of the national commission by filing an application within thirty days of the date of the order in question.

If the person so complaining had not been a party to the earlier proceeding, he would first be obliged to petition the regional commission for rehearing (within the same 30-day period) and would thereafter be free to seek national commission review. The timely filing of a petition for rehearing with the regional commission, or a petition for review with the national commission, would stay the time for seeking judicial review until such applications were disposed of by the respective commission. All final decisions of a regional commission would be subject to judicial review pursuant to the standards of the Administrative Procedure Act with venue lying in the United States Court of Appeals for the Circuit or Circuits in which the regional body is located providing that the review proceeding is begun within 60 days.

Thus before any person could challenge a regional commission order in the courts on the basis of its implications for other regions he would be obliged to bring his grievance to the national commission, which would either decline to accept review (in which case the order would become final) or set the matter for full hearing. From a procedural standpoint it might be provided that the national commission would be required to begin a review proceeding if any three of its commissioners so decided. From the standpoint of administrative convenience it might be desirable to delegate the actual review responsibility to a panel composed of three of the national commissioners—one from the regional commission whose order is under challenge, one from a region that allegedly will be affected by that order, and the third (and panel chairman) from a neutral region.

It is essential that the national and regional commissions be adequately staffed with the full range of expertise required to undertake the analytical efforts each will be called upon to complete. Financing can either be through general appropriated funds or by the imposition of a nationwide kilowatt hour surcharge. Monies should also support the creation of an independent public counsel to be established in each region to serve as counsel for environmental matters and for otherwise unrepresented consumers as appropriate before the regional commission, with full rights of appeal to the national commission and the courts.

In view of the complexity of the underlying issues, the public counsel must have available expertise to assure a full and independent exploration of all relevant issues. The participation of the public counsel in any proceeding would not exclude any other interested member of the public. Efforts should be made to encourage such public participation by the removal of cost obstacles that now often present insuperable barriers—for example, by the free availability of transcripts and the possibility that expert witness and attorney fees would be reimbursed where the regional commission concluded that the testimony or participation contributed to the preparation of a complete record.

In sum, the object of our proposal is to create a comprehensive forum for decision making that would facilitate participation by, and accountability to, the public. These regional authorities would lead to a more competitive industry structure, eventually placing greater reliance on the operation of market forces.

Chapter Six

Restructuring the Electric Power Industry

CONCENTRATION AND COMPETITION

The electric power industry has been moving toward concentration over the past several decades. In 1945 there were approximately 4,051 electric utilities in operation in the United States (1,060 of which were privately owned). Today the number is less than 3,500 with perhaps fewer than 300 privately owned systems remaining. For the most part the industry is vertically integrated. That is, a single entity produces (generates), transmits and distributes electricity. In addition, most utilities are interconnected with neighboring utilities.

In view of the existence of vertical integration we question the appropriateness of further concentrations of corporate control (for example, through mergers). Indeed, our legal system requires that horizontal competition be protected and furthered wherever possible. It is particularly important that interutility competition for customer loads be promoted in the electric power industry. The desire to achieve the efficient allocation of resources and to stimulate technological innovation demands no less.[a] The concentration of corporate control is eroding the opportunities that do exist for competition within the industry. While it is true that electric utilities are operating largely as

---

[a]It is well to keep in mind that regulation is not intended to displace competition. In passing upon the propriety of a bank merger the Supreme Court has noted (*United States v. Philadelphia National Bank*, 374 U.S. 321, 321 (1962)):

> ... that the forces of competition be allowed to operate within the broad framework of government regulation of the industry. The fact that banking is a highly regulated industry critical to the Nation's welfare makes the play of competition not less important but more so. . . . Subject to narrow qualifications, it is surely the case that competition is our fundamental national economic policy, offering as it does the only alternative to the cartelization or government regimentation of large portions of the economy. . . .

See also *United States v. El Paso Natural Gas*, 376 U.S. 651 (1964).

protected monopolies they have competed for wholesale sales, industrial sales, new service areas, and public acceptability ("yardstick" competition).

Wholesale sales—that is, purchases of electricity by a utility for ultimate resale—are common throughout the industry. In view of economy dispatch or shared savings arrangements and the near certainty that any system (as a consequence of an unscheduled outage) will find itself short of capacity, every utility can expect at times to assume the role of purchaser. The overwhelming number of smaller utilities (predominantly publicly owned) rely most heavily on purchased power.

Strong regional and interregional transmission ties, in addition to recent antitrust pronouncements (principally the *Otter Tail* decision), suggest that smaller utilities should be assured a wider choice of wholesale power suppliers. However, as corporate control is merged and as generation and transmission capacity comes under the control of a few dominant utilities, the practical opportunities for wholesale competition are reduced. Indeed, one of the consequences of joint planning is that the major utilities in an area stagger their construction activities. Thus, at any particular time there may be only one utility with excess capacity available for sale to small wholesale customers.

Accordingly, although the wholesale customer is usually a high load factor customer, which improves the economic position of the seller enabling it to take fuller advantage of any economies of scale, the small utility which desperately requires an incremental supply of purchased power may have very little bargaining leverage. The antitrust laws, which are cumbersome and expensive to enforce by private entities, offer little practical comfort to smaller utilities experiencing an imminent power deficiency.

There should also be aggressive competition for industrial and commercial loads. While the potential for such competition is most obvious in the case of contiguous power suppliers, it is not necessarily limited by geographic location. With rising energy costs and recurring brownouts and voltage reductions, managements of industrial enterprises will consider power supply factors (both price and the quality or dependability of service) as they assess geographical areas for future industrial expansion. Where the distribution systems of two or more utilities are contiguous, the possibility of interface competition is apparent. This is particularly so where their distribution systems extend to the fringe of areas not yet extensively developed (this is the case with respect to the popular "new town" phenomenon).

Finally, we must not ignore the present and perhaps renewed relevance of yardstick competition. As regulatory commissions are inundated with repeated rate increase filings, as environmentalists attack the social consequences of utility operations, and as investors realize the long term realities of the erosion of earnings and escalating capital costs, the potential for comparative analysis becomes even more imperative. However, such analysis is possible only if the industry enjoys diversity in management philosophies and regulatory commissions can assess the performance of many distribution entities operating within the same general geographic area.[b]

The maintenance of effective regulation is another factor which militates strongly against the concentration of ownership. The undue concentration of control could well frustrate both federal and state (but, arguably, not regional) regulation. Under the existing regulatory scheme the FPC's jurisdiction extends only to wholesale sales which only represent a minor portion of total utility earnings. If a single vertically integrated utility dominates a region, the extent of its wholesale transactions (and therefore exposure to FPC regulation) is minimal and perhaps nonexistent. The absence of FPC supervision will have prejudicial consequences at the local level. Generally, state commission staff resources are severely limited. Therefore, in their regulation of retail activities, state commissions rely heavily on the guidance supplied by FPC regulation of wholesale sales. Without such sales, and therefore without FPC guidance, the ability of state commissions to cope with the regulatory problems presented by large vertically integrated utilities will often be overwhelming.

Moreover, if utility operations are multistate in nature, individual state commissions will be confronted with complex cost allocation problems that would serve to frustrate their regulation of even activities which are intrastate in character. It could also impair regulatory supervision of bulk power supply planning and erode the inherent advantages of local management in what essentially is a service industry.

Vertical Integration

The adoption of a regional commission system of regulation would overcome these difficulties to a considerable extent, particularly if the new regulatory entities have the resources required to enable them to analyze in detail the activities of regulated firms. The restructuring of regulation alone, however, would not achieve the advantages of more aggressive interutility competition and of management diversity. A complementary restructuring of industry is required—a restructuring that would end vertical integration by separating generation and transmission from distribution.

Effective regional pooling would offer the benefits of differing management philosophies but it would not resolve the problems of vertical

---

[b]As Professor Leonard Weiss observed in the AEP-Columbus and Southern proceeding (Justice Department Exhibit 220, p. 10):

> Finally, regulatory personnel are in constant contact with the utilities within their own state and have much less contact with those in other states. They are likely to be particularly influenced by local experience in setting criteria for "prudent costs," "reasonable return" or "reasonable rates" when they try to determine what rates are most appropriate within their jurisdictions. If the state regulatory authorities are faced by only one or a few utilities they will have few relevant criteria. It is not easy to determine which costs are unavoidable and which are unnecessary. The existence of a variety of utilities against which decisions for any one can be tested probably makes regulation more effective.

integration. Indeed, they may even be exacerbated through the introduction of horizontal restraints (which may only be implicit) among pool participants. For example, a smaller utility which wants to participate in the ownership of a new, large base-load unit understandably may shy away from interface competition with the project's major owners. It is inescapable that pooling fosters collusion; this is particularly significant when the collaborators are vertically integrated monopolies.

Further, the very existence of the merger possibility may stand as an inhibition to joint planning and coordination. If a small investor owned utility is denied the rate base advantages inherent in joint participation, its financial stability could well be impaired, making it a prime target for takeover. While rate base erosion considerations are of little or no relevance in the case of consumer owned systems, if they are denied access to new efficient units, and made to pay a less attractive rate for purchased power with a corresponding inability to compete for new growth, it is conceivable that acquisition overtures by privately owned suppliers will be difficult to resist, particularly where the local population witnesses discriminatory (as between wholesale and retail customer classes) pricing.

Consistent with the prejudice of our national antitrust policy, vertical integration must be precluded unless the proponents of vertical integration can demonstrate that its benefits outweigh the implicit prejudice. They have not yet even been asked to do so. With lingering visions of the truly local utility, the nation has passively accepted the logic of tying together under a single corporate umbrella production, transmission and distribution activities.

But this merger of separable functions unnecessarily reduces competition and strains both the utilities and society. It is easy enough to understand why the industry would develop along those lines as individual, isolated central station service systems were placed in operation almost a century ago. But today the industry is, for the most part, fully integrated and generation sources are often far removed from load centers. Each utility is under pressure to become a bulk power supplier either as a means of securing access to newer, more efficient generating forms thereby permitting it to compete for loads, or as a demonstration of its ability to keep pace with industry counterparts. As long as utilities are subjected to rate base regulation and compete in the same capital market, this psychological factor cannot be dismissed. Yet the availability of the technical expertise required for the operational management of the new complex units is limited.

Moreover, acceptable sites are not to be found in each and every utility back yard. Nevertheless it is often the case that utilities are required (in some cases legally; in many more because of practical corporate limitations) to locate facilities close to their service areas. In view of the promised advances in extra high voltage transmission any such locational limitations must be questioned.[c] The prognosis for high capacity (superconducting, cryogenic) underground transmission is most encouraging for the decades of the 1980s and 90s. Once a basic national grid is installed (analogous to our interstate highway system) it should be possible to locate bulk power supply facilities almost without regard for their proximity to load centers. The industry will also have a far greater ability to take advantage of regional load diversity, thereby lessening the total national requirements for generating capacity.

If bulk power plants are to be further divorced from load centers—as they most certainly will be if the nation moves in the direction of off-shore nuclear islands—and are to be under the operational management of technical specialists (as many joint projects already are), it is difficult to justify the vertical integration of production and distribution activities.

The siting and operation of mammoth new power plant installations and extra high voltage networks has demanded technical expertise in planning and decision making not previously required, as well as management skills different from those which have been essential to the operation of even the larger distribution systems. Indeed, the continuation of vertical integration would lead to management inefficiency by requiring the retention of technicians whose skills are not needed in the operation of distribution systems. In this respect the merger of production and distribution activities has even less to support it than does the merger of electric and natural gas distribution activities. Yet even those economies are considered by many to be minimal and more than offset by the competitive disadvantages.

The only conceivable justification for vertical integration, therefore, is the need to provide an opportunity for capital expansion in view of the dependence on rate base regulation. This justification is insufficient on several counts. First, if distribution companies do not build future generation and transmission facilities they will not need an ever increasing source of capital finance (a need occasioned by high cost capacity additions). Therefore, there is no need for an expanding rate base. Second, as already pointed out, regulators are not tied to rate base methodologies. Ample economic rewards can be bestowed upon distribution entities regardless of the static, or even diminishing, nature of their capital plants. Third, if rate base expansion is considered important, construction of underground local distribution lines and the installation of equipment to facilitate peak load pricing will afford distribution companies ample opportunities to increase their capital investments. At the distribution level it generally is accepted that economies of scale are not dependent on the total utility load once it achieves a fairly modest size.

---

[c]See *Underground Power Transmission*, a study prepared by Arthur D. Little, Inc. for the Electric Research Council (October 1971), and *FCST Energy R & D Goals Study*, a Report of the Federal Technical Group on Electrical Transmission and Systems (July 14, 1972).

In sum, we argue that generation and transmission functions should be separated from distribution. Favoring diversity, and concerned about undue concentration, we would favor the creation of multiple regional power suppliers, each of which would be certificated by a supervising regulatory authority (our regional commissions or the FPC). In this way it would be possible to achieve the benefits of competition (including yardstick competition), a preferred position in the capital market, and the availability of the highly trained technical experts so essential to the planning and daily operation of sophisticated generation and transmission facilities. Even this degree of concentration poses problems. It will only be tolerable if the supervising regulatory authority (and the public counsel we urge be established) has sufficient independent expertise (financial as well as technical) to undertake a complete independent review of company presentations.

Natural Gas Industry Experience

In the case of the natural gas industry, separation of production and distribution functions may well have contributed to the current shortage situation. Natural gas production companies, being highly diversified international operations, dedicate their capital where the return appears most promising; thus natural gas exploration may suffer as a consequence. We would protect against the repetition of this difficulty in the electric power industry by prohibiting any diversification by generation and transmission entities.

The ability of the smaller, independent natural gas producers to have a significant impact on supply has lessened considerably as production moved to offshore areas. In view of the Interior Department's leasing procedures (which require the payment of bonus amounts for large tracts of land well before any production can commence) and the high cost of drilling offshore, it apparently is difficult even for the major oil companies to operate offshore without joining together in drilling combines.

With the separation of distribution entities, the ability of state commissions to discharge their regulatory functions should be enhanced markedly. The separation of generation and transmission activities from distribution would remove most of the complex allocation problems that now often overwhelm commissions, particularly at the state level. In short, effective regulation should be promoted on all levels while securing the benefits of local management and maximizing competitive diversity particularly in the area of ultimate consumer service. This separation is not entirely novel, even in this country. It is the situation that prevails in large parts of the Bonneville and Tennessee Valley Authority service areas. Further, it is the pattern followed in Great Britain and in parts of Canada.

We are not alone in recommending a realignment of the electric power industry. In a 1970 report prepared for the New England Regional Commission it was concluded that "the best ultimate answer for New England is a single bulk power supply agency with full responsibility for the generation and transmission of electric power."[d] As conceived, the new agency would have sole authority to construct future generation and transmission facilities, possibly subject to some separate site certification authority, and might or might not begin by the acquisition of existing facilities as well. As alternative models the report suggests "a multi-state agency or a private corporation, perhaps with federal involvement along the lines of the Comsat precedent" (pp. 21-22), and a regional site acquisition authority patterned after the New York Space and Atomic Development Agency, which is charged with the acquisition of nuclear power plant sites in that state. The regional agency would make payments in lieu of taxes to state and local governments and would be excused from the need to comply with the licensing requirements of state or federal environmental standard setting agencies.

We have already addressed our objections to the merger of environmental standard setting and licensing responsibilities. As to the matter of taxes, we agree that payments should be made to local authorities as compensation for lost tax base. Persons who reside in the vicinity of generation and transmission facilities will bear most of the brunt of external costs and these also should be compensated. Reduced property taxes would appear to be a politically acceptable form for such payment. While it may be that one would be hard pressed to find a taxpayer who is not also a consumer of electricity we do not all consume at the same level. Second, removing local tax base would surely impose a significant additional siting obstacle.

More recently, Huettner and Landon have proposed that the electric power industry be reconstituted so as to parallel the structure of the natural gas industry—that is, by the creation of separate production, transmission, and distribution segments.[e] Except in remote areas, no vertical integration would be permitted. The generation segment would be deregulated; the transmission segment would be placed under somewhat expanded FPC regulatory control; and the distribution segment would remain subject to local regulation. It is assumed that the generation segment would become competitive and would sell its output to distribution entities pursuant to long term (five-year) contracts. In securing supplies, distributors would seek competitive bids from the independent producers. Transmission entities would be required to operate as common carriers accessible to all producers and distributors.

We do not agree with the willingness, as expressed in the New England report, to concentrate responsibility for future power supply in a single

---

[d]*A Study of the Electric Power Industry in New England 1970-1990,* The New England Regional Commission, September 1970, p. 16.

[e]David A. Huettner and John H. Landon, *Restructuring the Electric Utility Industry: An Economic Analysis,* presented at the Seminar on Problems of Regulation and Public Utilities, Amos Tuck School of Business Administration, Dartmouth College, August 29, 1973.

entity, public or private. We are committed to the view that regulation is not a substitute for competition and that management diversity is essential to the achievement of optimal efficiency, particularly in an industry beset by novel economic, technical, and social difficulties and facing a wide spectrum of future options.

Power Production Competition

We share the Huettner/Landon predisposition toward the stimulation of a competitive thrust at least in the power production segment. The argument that electric utilities are "natural monopolies" is based, insofar as generation is concerned, on the existence of economies of scale. There is, however, a limit to economies of scale which tends to stimulate competition among several generating firms within each region. Present indications are that most economies of scale are reached at about the 600 mw level and few persons are optimistic about technological breakthroughs over the next decade which will serve to significantly push that level up. In view of the fact that the optimal unit size may be quite moderate (particularly if there is a desire to reduce reserve requirements which must contemplate the loss of the largest unit), new entry by smaller firms is quite likely, providing guaranteed access to the transmission grid exists. Indeed, the existing technological fix may make new entry by independent firms a natural (rather than legislatively required) phenomenon.

We cannot accept either their implicit assumption in favor of free entry or their sanctioning of total deregulation in generation. They recognize that with free entry, the bankruptcy of generating companies will be expected occurrences. Generation companies, particularly new entrants, either because of their inability to cope with rising capital costs or construction delays, or because of their desire to win supply contracts, will be induced to offer bids which are unrealistically low which in turn will hamper their ability to fulfill contractual commitments. Huettner and Landon assume that a combination of performance bonds and the existence of adequate reserves (presumably available from other generation entities) will adequately protect both the distribution company and its ultimate consumers. We do not agree. To be sure, performance bonds, warranties, long term contracts, and similar devices—including perhaps a form of "futures market" in generating capacity—may be used to foster market stability. The critical position of the electric power industry in the economy requires that these be complemented by regulatory guarantees of adequate electrical supply.

A distribution entity would most likely contract with its sole wholesale supplier for a desired reserve margin in order to avoid the economic penalty associated with being a low load factor customer of a second supplier. Presumably this difficulty could be lessened by each bulk power supplier agreeing to serve as a reserve (or backup) supplier for the customers of a competitive producer. But it is difficult to conceive of this possibility if the industry is truly competitive. Moreover, we are hesitant to sanction the need for what easily could be collusive arrangements particularly since under the Huettner/Landon model the power supply segment would be unregulated. We also suspect that this procedure would serve to exacerbate reserve requirements resulting in related economic and environmental costs.

We therefore cannot agree that the bulk power supply segment should be freed of federal (or regional) regulation. Perhaps after experience is gained under the intermediate step we offer, such a suggestion would be worthy of consideration. But there must be the assurance that there would be active competition between relatively equal contenders for wholesale business, and wholesale customers must in fact have access to competing suppliers through a nationwide high voltage transmission network. While the possibility exists that such a network could be developed following perfection of now experimental underground transmission technologies, it is premature to assume free access in advance of the availability of a transportation system in place.

Deregulation of bulk power suppliers could introduce a new measure of unaccountability. Free market competition can be effective in maximizing efficiency, where the measure of efficiency is confined to private costs. But in the case of electric power plant siting and operation it is not adequate to be concerned with "price" competition alone; our current problems are due in part to a failure to recognize externalities or social costs. Such factors cannot easily be worked into a system governed solely by marketplace competition. This could be particularly true when the bulk power supply, having no direct service dealings with ultimate consumers, has no direct public accountability.

It might be possible to partially offset this failure to account for externalities by having a public agency develop a social dollar cost for each bulk power supply site. Should a supplier wish to construct on that site it would have to pay a tax equivalent to the assigned social cost or, alternatively, make an equivalent contribution into an externality fund. Since these added costs would have to be reflected as production expenses, there would be incentive to minimize them by selecting sites that bring with them the least externalities. Even if dollars are not transferred it is important to develop a site bidding system that includes social as well as private cost considerations. However, even this partial response requires site regulation, at a minimum. The operation of "social cost" regulation beside a competitive industry structure is not without precedent. It certainly applies in the case of the drug and consumer products industries through the existence of the Food and Drug Administration and the Consumer Product Safety Commission.

Under the Huettner/Landon model state regulation would continue for distribution entities but competitive bidding alone would, from the outset, govern the wholesale price of electricity. This total absence of regulatory review on the bulk power level would introduce several complications, however. In view of construction lead times, supply contracts would have to be let five to seven years in advance of actual production. When is the local commission to regulate this element of distribution expense? If it is to take place at the time bids are solicited and accepted, regulation will be meaningless.

The industry has not been able to realize anticipated power supply costs. If the costs escalate dramatically during the construction period, or local regulatory review is postponed until the capacity is on line, there would be little opportunity for meaningful rate oversight. It is unlikely that distributors would be able to find alternative sources of supply at that late date. Indeed, it is quite likely that bulk power suppliers will require price escalation clauses as a hedge against unanticipated cost increases.

While it is fine to argue that they should be made to compete on a firm price basis, to do so will either magnify the bankruptcy problem, inhibit free entry, or result in higher contingency margins in all bids. Regional commission regulation of entry through the comparative analysis approach would afford a more meaningful opportunity to assess cost projections. Most important, it would overcome the social problems that arise when competition only addresses private costs. Without regulatory review it does not appear possible to insure that competition alone would encourage the minimization of externalities.

We accept the proposition that the transmission segment, whether or not it is separated from production and distribution, should be converted to common carrier status. However, this can be accomplished under the present industry structure and we believe it should be, whether or not more basic structural alterations are pursued. For example, all extra high voltage transmission facilities (say 230 Kv and above) could be placed under comprehensive FPC jurisdiction. Capacity in excess of the short, intermediate, or long term needs of its owner would be available, pursuant to FPC regulation, for use by any generation and transmission entity.

Contracts for a specified term would be tariffs filed with the Commission. Further, any utility should be free to expand, at its own expense, the transmission capability of another utility's corridor, either by upgrading the capacity or capability of existing facilities or adding circuits where feasible, or paralleling with new facilities, providing that it does not unduly impair the operations of the owner utility and that such owner is compensated for all reasonable costs (possibly including lost options) it will suffer.

By "free to expand" we mean pursuant to an application filed with, and approved by, the FPC. It is our expectation that many of the advantages of common carrier status could be achieved through pooling and more aggressive FPC coordination and rate review initiatives. Certainly the realization of these objectives would be a prime responsibility of the regional commissions as they develop regional coordination plans.

However, there are arguments that can be made for retaining the merger of the generation and transmission segments. Their separation would introduce several practical problems. How would a generation entity be able to plan its expansion program, with its seven to ten year lead time, if it has no control over the availability of transmission? How can distributors solicit bids from producers without integrating transmission availability and cost considerations? How is a producer to practice economy dispatch without control over the transmission network? And how do you account for the fact that power flow cannot be routed with precision over any particular path particularly in the event of an unexpected outage?

The natural gas analogy is not fully applicable. A natural gas producer, if denied access to a pipeline transportation system, simply caps the well and bears relatively nominal carrying costs. The economic penalty that would have to be borne by a generation entity denied access to a transmission system capable of serving its loads (if only because excess capacity is not available) would be disastrous. Also, sharing reserve requirements is a necessary condition for the future electric power industry. Technical failures in the electric power industry are quite different from natural gas production shortfalls.

Thus far we have avoided the recurring debate over the appropriateness of affording public power systems the preferential treatment inherent in federal or tax free financing. Without belaboring the point our initial prejudice is against subsidies, particularly where they are exacted from the public generally in favor of a more limited consuming group. However, in past years those subsidies were essential to accomplish an overriding social objective: to bring the advantages of power to large segments of the population not being served by the private sector. It was also important to develop an economic yardstick.

Today, as our concern shifts more toward issues of social accountability, the importance of the yardstick concept remains and perhaps enjoys new prominence. It should be noted, moreover, that the economic advantages do not flow only to the public power sector. Rural electrification funds were never limited to cooperatives. Private utilities were free to apply and receive them. The only limiting condition was that REA financing was limited to supplying service to rural areas. Today privately owned utilities are making increasing use of public tax free financing through the issuance of pollution control bonds. By the end of 1972, there were 52 such bond issues averaging $11 million apiece.[f]

Obviously the presence in every region of a strong federal marketing agency (if its influence were properly directed) could go a long way toward securing regional coordination objectives as Bonneville has accomplished in the Pacific Northwest. Such a federal presence would also help secure the continued vitality of small investor owned and public systems that are now at the mercy of single source suppliers. Finally, the yardstick influence of regional marketing agencies could be most significant, particularly if those agencies are committed to sound environmental management. For these reasons, and in view of the need for a bulk power supplier willing to implement a regional scenario, should the

---

[f]See John Winders, "Tax-Free Anti-Pollution IRB's Head Toward 1 Billion Dollars in '73," *The Bond Buyer*, March 14, 1973.

private entrants decline so to do, we would hope that one of the regional suppliers under our proposal would be publicly owned. In several cases this would easily be accomplished by simply reconstituting existing federal marketing agencies.

INTERACTION

A final comment about the interaction of our proposed regulatory and industry restructuring. We recognize that we may well be replacing vertical monopolies with several giant production combines. However, the assumed prejudice of this arrangement would be largely offset by the presence of an independent public bulk power supplier and the creation of an effective regulatory mechanism. Moreover, it would not be necessary to forego the advantages that may accrue to a distributor (and to society generally) from being able to obtain a power supply from a producer in a remote region.

As part of its planning function each regional commission, working through the National Coordinating Commission, would be expected to maximize the benefits of time diversity by requiring that the alternative of purchasing from outside of the region be substituted for expansion of regional capacity. Hopefully, the entire nation will thereby share the benefits of reduced social and private costs, as would occur where a region makes use of far distant geothermal capacity in lieu of adding its own peaking facilities.

Appendixes

Appendix A

Defining and Measuring the Price Elasticity of Demand for Electricity

Debates over the appropriate level of consumption of electric power or its rate of growth as well as the problem of revenue erosion depend to a considerable extent on the economic concept of price elasticity. This term is most easily understood by considering the following expression:

$$
\begin{array}{ccccc}
\text{Percent Change} & = & \text{Percent Change} & + & \text{Percent Change} & \text{(A.1)} \\
\text{in} & & \text{in Quantity} & & \text{in Price} \\
\text{Total Revenue} & & & &
\end{array}
$$

$$
(\% \Delta \text{TR}) \quad = \quad (\% \Delta Q) \quad + \quad (\% \Delta P)
$$

Equation (1) states that the percentage change in price plus the percentage change in quantity sold equals the percentage change in total revenue. A cornerstone of consumer demand theory is the notion that the more one consumes of any commodity the less he will be willing to pay for additional units of it. Economists use a demand function to describe such an inverse relationship between the quantity demanded and its price. Therefore, moving along a demand schedule or function as price increases, quantity demanded will decline and vice versa.

A good that is totally insensitive to price is called perfectly price inelastic and has a zero price elasticity. Changing price would not affect the quantity of the good demanded, but it would affect total revenue. The consumption of most commodities is believed to be sensitive to price and a price

This appendix was prepared with the help of Professor V. Kerry Smith of the Department of Economics at the State University of New York at Binghamton. It is based upon portions of a jointly authored paper: V.K. Smith, C.J. Cicchetti, and W.J. Gillen, "Electric Power Regulation Externalities and the A-J-W Effect," presented at the Seminar on Problems of Regulation and Public Utilities, The Amos Tuck School of Business Administration, Dartmouth College, August 1973.

increase will, it follows, cause the quantity consumed to decline. Such offsetting effects will determine the new total revenue. In fact, if percentage price increase exceeds the percentage quantity decrease, total revenue will increase, and vice versa for a price decrease.

A situation like this would occur, if the price elasticity of demand was inelastic—that is, its value was between 0 and minus one (-1). On the other hand, if the price elasticity of demand had an absolute value greater than unity, then with a price increase a percentage change in price would be more than offset by the percent decline in quantity demanded and total revenue would decline, and vice versa, for a price decrease. Table A-1 summarizes these effects.

If one is concerned about assessing the implication of price increases, whether it be for determining the effect on the quantity consumed or the firm's total revenue, the price elasticity of demand is a most important factor. In the past electric utilities and commission staffs generally assumed the price elasticity of demand for electricity to be zero. The asymmetry between the effects of a price increase and a price decrease is important in this regard. During the postwar period of price and cost decline, this assumption of zero price elasticity meant that expected revenue calculations would be underestimated if price elasticity was nonzero, since no adjustments were made for any increase in volume attributable to the price decrease. During the present period of price increases this practice causes a revenue shortfall, puts additional strains on the regulatory commission, and is likely to cause a downgrading in the firm's financial rating. The reason for this is that if price increases cause a reduction in consumption as a nonzero price elasticity would imply, then the company would not earn the revenue requirements approved by the regulatory commission, since the loss in volume attributable to the price increase would not be taken into account.

Environmentalists, who are concerned about the impact of an expanded generation and transmission system, view the price elasticity of demand for electricity as an important parameter. Most future expansion plans

Table A-1. The Effect of Price Elasticity on Total Revenue

Price Elasticity (Absolute Value)	Price Change	Quantity Change	Effect on Total Revenue
Equal 0	increase	no change	increase
	decrease	no change	decrease
Less than 1	increase	decrease	increase
	decrease	increase	decrease
Equals 1	increase	decrease	no change
	decrease	increase	no change
Greater than 1	increase	decrease	decrease
	decrease	increase	increase

are based upon "need" projections that are themselves based upon growth rates taken from a period of declining electric prices. To the extent that the future appears to be a period of rising prices, environmentalists would like to see a downward adjustment in future consumption estimates and therefore in facility "need" forecasts.

Price elasticity of demand is also an important parameter if the various pricing rules of economists discussed elsewhere in the text are to be implemented by regulatory commissions in an objective manner. Allocating revenue requirements among the various customer categories involves both equity and efficiency considerations, and price elasticity estimates for various types of use and categories of customers are most important decision making parameters.

From a revenue, environmental, equity, and economic efficiency standpoint, the price elasticity of demand is an important parameter. However, attempts to measure this important parameter have brought about some confusion in the minds of regulatory commissions, utilities and intervenors. The main purpose of the following discussion is to untangle these matters. As a first step, the empirical price elasticities studies that have been undertaken for the United States are reviewed below.

PREVIOUS STUDIES OF THE DEMAND
FOR ELECTRIC POWER[a]

The first major study of the demand for electric power was conducted by Fisher and Kaysen.[b] Their demand models for the household component of electricity demand were assumed to be related to the stock of appliances and their rates of use. Both time series data for the 48 states and pooled data for groups of states were employed to estimate household demand relationships. For industry demand, the estimates were based upon industrial firms (two digit SIC) for 1956. There was very little additional work in the ensuing decade.

More recently, a cross-sectional analysis of 77 cities by Wilson was conducted.[c] He was critical of both the Fisher-Kaysen approach and data. His conclusions suggest that price is the primary determinant of the volume of electricity consumed. Moreover, in contrast to Fisher-Kaysen, Wilson finds the residential demand to be price elastic. Finally, Wilson found that the price of a competing energy source, natural gas, also is significant. Wilson used two price

---

[a]This review is based on a paper written by V. Kerry Smith, and two of the present authors for the 1973 Amos Tuck Institute, "Electric Power Regulation, Externalities and A-J-W Effect."

[b]F.M. Fisher and C. Kaysen, *The Demand for Electricity in the United States*, North Holland, Amsterdam, 1962.

[c]J.W. Wilson, "Residential Demand for Electricity," *Quarterly Review of Economics and Business*, 11, 7-22 (1971) and *Residential and Industrial Demand for Electricity*, unpublished Ph.D. thesis, Cornell University, 1969.

measures, average revenue and the FPC's typical bill for 500 kilowatt hours per month, but reports the results only for the latter. Mount, Chapman, and Tyrrell;[d] Anderson;[e] and Halvorsen[f] have also recently published analyses of the demand for electricity. Anderson analyzed the demand for the residential market using a 1969 cross-section of the states, and a time series sample for California from 1947 to 1969. Mount, Chapman, and Tyrrell analyzed the demand for residential, commercial and industrial classes using a pooled time series cross-section sample for the 48 states from 1946 to 1970. Halvorsen's study is also based upon a pooled sample for the 48 states from 1961 to 1969, and focuses upon residential demand.

These studies may be distinguished according to (1) their price measures, (2) attention given to the "identification problem," (3) concern with possible simultaneous equations bias, (4) the estimation procedure used, and (5) consideration of cross elasticities of demand. Fisher and Kaysen use average revenue, but are fully cognizant of its relationship to the quantity of electricity as a result of the declining block rates, which generally characterize the pricing of electricity. They note that the average price per kilowatt hour is not the marginal price of economic theory, and is not unrelated to the number of kilowatt hours consumed in a given time period. However, they suggest that:

1. To the extent not all consumers in the same state are subject to the same block rates, the importance of a difference between average and marginal price will be reduced.

2. To the extent customers tend to move into different steps in their rate schedules and that the mix of customers change, the difference will be less important.

3. The relationship between quantity and price from the block rate schedules relates to money price, and the real price is what is relevant to the demand schedule, so that

> over time, the rate schedule relationship between the real price of electricity and the amount of electricity used can be expected to be almost nonexistent, whatever is the case for the relationship with money price. This is so because the rate schedules tend to remain fairly constant while the price index shifts through time.

It should be further noted that if any bias remains from using average rather than marginal prices, its direction is easy to understand. Since

---

[d]F.D. Mount, L.D. Chapman, and T.J. Tyrrell, "Elasticity Demand in the United States: An Econometric Analysis," ORNL-NSF-EP-49, June 1973.

[e]K.P. Anderson, "The Demand for Electricity: Econometric Estimates for California and the United States," RAND R-905-NSF, Santa Monica, California, 1972.

[f]R. Halvorsen, "Residential Electricity: Demand and Supply," presented at the Sierra Club Conference on Power and Public Policy, Vermont, January 1972.

marginal prices are always less than or equal to average prices, average price based price elasticity estimates will be biased upward in absolute value.

Wilson and Anderson suggest that use of the typical bill as a measure of marginal price reduces the simultaneity problem. However, the typical bill is related to the quantity selected and therefore, the mix of customers around the quantity representing the basis for the typical bill is important to its value as a price measure. Apparently Mount, Chapman, and Tyrrell are not concerned with the simultaneity problem. They use average revenue as a price measure in real terms and focus their attention upon estimating demand when there is a lagged endogenous variable and potential serial correlation. Rather than adjust the estimator to reflect their assumed error structure, these authors replace the lagged quantity variable (which is essential to their short run-long run distinction in elasticity estimates) with an instrument, and perform instrumental variable estimation as well as orindary least squares.

Halvorsen's study formulates a simultaneous equation model and uses two stage least squares to estimate residential demand. Explicit specification of the determinants of the average revenue from residential sales in nominal terms serves to identify demand through exclusion restrictions. All other authors use ordinary least squares methods for estimating demand relationships. None of the authors tests for intertemporal or across market links in demand.

Table A-2 presents the range of elasticity estimates as reported in each of these studies. One overall observation which seems consistent with the existing empirical work is that the industrial class of customer's demand is most elastic, with commercial somewhat less elastic, and residential less elastic than commercial. There is, however, some overlap between the range of estimates for the different categories and comparisons between studies is hazardous.

There have also been two examples of statewide price elasticity estimation that have been employed in electric utility regulatory proceedings. The first was presented in a "rough and ready" form by Cicchetti[g] in a case before the Wisconsin Public Service Commission. He used pooled cross-sectional utility and time series data. In response to initial criticism from the utilities' economic consultants, the National Economic Research Associates, revised estimation procedures were undertaken to account for simultaneous equations bias, autocorrelation and heteroscedasticity. These were presented to the commission in a supplemental testimony that used two-stage least squares, an error components model and a combined two-stage and generalized least squares approach for residential, commercial, and industrial categories.

In testimony before the New York Public Service Commission, V.K. Smith reported results of price elasticity estimates derived for the various utilities in New York by himself and Cicchetti.[h] In New York the utility data

---

[g]See testimony of Charles J. Cicchetti, In the Matter of Madison Gas and Electric Application for a Rate Increase; Wisconsin Public Service Commission, Docket: 2U 7423.

[h]See testimony of V. Kerry Smith, In the Matter of Niagara Mohawk Application for a Rate Increase; New York Public Service Commission, Case: 26402.

Table A-2.   Price Elasticity Estimates from Various Empirical Studies

Author	Date of Data	Class	Range of Price Elasticities[a]	Additional Remarks
Fisher-Kaysen (1962)	1946-1957	Residential Two-Digit Industrial	.22 to .99	Uses first difference variables for time series models for households and average revenue for price
Wilson (1971)	Cross-section of 77 cities (1968?)	Residential	1.33	Uses FPC's typical bill for 500 kilowatt hours per month as price
Anderson (1972)	Cross-section of states in 1969; 1947-1969 Calif.	Residential	.84 to .90 for cross-section	Uses change in typical bill from 500/kwh/month to 1000/kwh/month as price and average revenue for study of California
Halvorsen (1972)	Moving cross-section of 48 states 1961-69	Residential	1.14 (2SLS) 1.09 (OLS) 1.16 with respect to marginal price	Uses a three equation simultaneous equation model to forecast demand; average revenue is used for price

Mount, Chapman	Moving cross-section of 48 states 1946-1970	Residential
		Commercial
		Industrial
			Short Run
			R (.09–.15 (OLS))
			  (.25–.27 (IV))
			C (.10–.13 (OLS))
			  (.71–.81 (IV))
			I (.12–.16 (OLS))
			  (.80–1.08 (IV))
			Long Run
			R (.76–1.00 (OLS))
			  (.87–.96 (IV))
			C (.80–1.04 (OLS))
			  (.87–.99 (IV))
			I (.99–1.27 (OLS))
			  (1.02–1.38 (IV))
				Uses average revenue as price variable

[a]These are the range of estimates which enable the rejection of the null hypothesis of no association. All are stated as positive numbers but each had the appropriate minus sign.

were not pooled, but a two-stage least squares technique was employed. In addition, commercial and industrial data was combined and cross and inter-temporal price effects were considered. Both studies found empirical parameters that were consistent with those reported in Table A-2 by the other researchers.

THE IDENTIFICATION PROBLEM

In empirical work the economist does not generally have the freedom of inquiry that physical and biological scientists have. For example, the social scientist cannot generally experiment and hold all factors that will affect a result constant while varying the one in question. Highly developed mathematical economic models hold other things constant, but when attempts are made to estimate the parameters of these mathematical models, the real world data may not be so cooperative as the calculus.

The problem of untangling observed data in order to test hypotheses of specific mathematical expressions of economic theory is known as the "identification problem." Since demand price and supply price are identical in a given market equilibrium at the same time that the quantity consumed equals the quantity demanded and supplied at this equilibrium, it is difficult to untangle observed price and quantity data to determine a separate demand and/or supply function. Figure A-1 illustrates this problem. Unlike the normal upward sloping supply schedule of most industries, the downward sloped schedule is used due to the declining rate block pricing of electric utilities. The declining rate block pricing practice should not be confused with the identification problem.

The functions labeled DAP_l and DAP_h are the low and high demand schedules over the period of observation, and SAP_l and SAP_h are the low and high declining rate block price or supply schedules. Market data on prices and quantity are represented by the smaller intersections that are shown within this region of upper and lower bound demand and supply schedules. Whether these observations can be used to estimate a demand or supply schedule depends upon what other information is available to the analyst.

For example, if variations across geographic regions in price sched-ules are greater than expected variations in demand (after accounting for other factors that might influence demand), then this information can be used to identify a demand schedule. This has been the implicit motivation behind the cross-section, time series, and pooled data estimates used in the various price elasticity studies mentioned above. Declining rate block price schedules affect the method of approaching the identification problem, but they should not be confused with the problem itself, nor be regarded as an unsolvable stumbling block.

Econometricians have several techniques that they utilize to identify economic relationships from observed data. Sometimes the technique requires

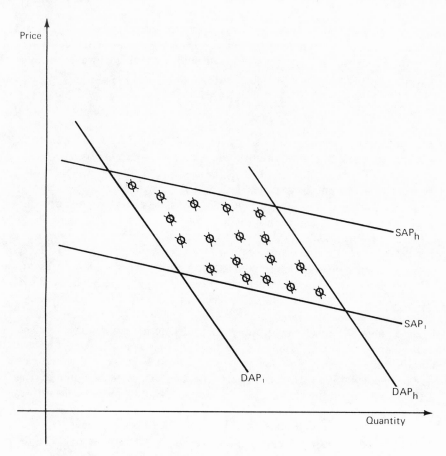

Figure A-1. Typical Market Observations of Average Prices and Quantity Consumed

that the analyst turn to estimating techniques that involve more intricate calculations than ordinary least squares. On the other hand more complicated data gathering that reduces the number of simultaneously varying economic factors will generally mean that less intricate estimation procedures may succeed. Since price elasticity is a most important parameter for the utility, regulatory commission, and intervenor alike, we recommend continued empirical work to further improve both the underlying data base and estimating procedures. However, it must be emphasized that to ignore the general consensus that "price matters" is not neutral. Instead, continuing to assume that the price elasticity of demand is zero means that there will be revenue erosion, continuing rate proceedings, and forecasts of need that are excessive.

We further recommend:

1. That research into the capacity of industrial firms to take advantage of low off peak prices be undertaken.
2. That experiments be attempted to discover the way residential customers would react to on peak and off peak price differentials.
3. As part of 2 that various price metering schemes be analyzed in order to guide regulatory commissions and utilities seeking to implement the pricing scheme.
4. That research into consumer demand according to energy using appliances employed and various energy sources available be undertaken, in light of some of the ongoing consumer expenditure surveys.

Price elasticity of demand is a most important parameter. Progress has been made in demonstrating this fact. Initial efforts have been made to estimate it using average prices and typical bills. The time to move beyond these initially important but crude estimates to more refined and less qualified ones has arrived. An objective solution to the current electric utility industry's pricing-earnings problems requires no less.

Appendix B

Some Mathematics of Public Utility Pricing: A Synthesis of Marginal Cost Pricing, Regulatory Constraints, Averch-Johnson Bias, and Peak Load Pricing and Block Pricing

There has recently been considerable renewed interest in public utility pricing practices. The purpose of this discussion is to review the mathematical derivation and policy implications of various pricing guides. Both positive (firm behavior) and normative (welfare maximization) objectives will be analyzed. While much of what will follow is well known, a synthesis of the principle current pricing issues in regulatory economics and a comparison of their positive and normative formulations is in order. In all cases the analysis that follows will be partial equilibrium and problems of the second best will be omitted.

MARGINAL COST PRICING

The starting point of any economic pricing rule is marginal cost pricing. In order to demonstrate how the additional considerations that follow can be derived from this starting point a formal statement of an objective function is made and maximized.

Let

$$P = f(Q) \tag{B.1}$$

The work described is a synthesis of a very important literature. The analytical work is heavily borrowed from previous works, which are referenced in the accompanying footnotes. In addition, Paul Joskow, Kerry Smith, Paul Smolensky, and Ralph Turvey took the time to share some of their own unpublished work and to comment on earlier drafts of the paper. John Stewart and Scott Goldsmith, each of whom is writing a thesis in this area, contributed greatly both in a substantive way and in sustaining the interest in these matters—Charles J. Cicchetti and John L. Jurewitz are responsible for its contents.

where

P is society's willingness to pay for varying amounts of Q or output of a particular commodity

$f(Q)$ is the demand function

Welfare (W) is defined as the difference between what society is willing to pay or total benefits and the total social costs (SC) of producing the output. The demand function may be viewed as the marginal benefit function of society, therefore total benefits are defined as the integral of the demand function:

$$TB = \int PdQ \tag{B.2}$$

Since total social costs are also a function of output, Q, the welfare function can be stated as:

$$W = TB - SC \tag{B.3}$$

which becomes:

$$W = \int PdQ - g(Q) \tag{B.3'}$$

where

$g(Q)$ is the total social cost function.

Welfare defined in this way can be viewed as an objective function. Maximizing welfare yields the following necessary condition:

$$\frac{dW}{dQ} = P - \frac{dSC}{dQ} = P - g'(Q) = 0 \tag{B.4}$$

$$\therefore \qquad P = g'(Q) \tag{B.5}$$

Note that P is the price of the product and when welfare is maximized it is set equal to $g'(Q)$ or the marginal social cost.

The above development explains the pricing behavior of a social welfare maximizer and it is therefore a normative result. However, pricing rules are usually set by private firms, which are more likely to use a profit maximizing criteria rather than a welfare maximizing criteria. The analogous positive formulation may be derived as follows:

$$\Pi = PQ - TC \tag{B.6}$$

where

II is total profit

PQ is the total revenue of the firm, and

TC is its total cost, which may or may not be equal to the total social cost used in the normative derivation

Maximizing the positive objective function (B.6) yields the following necessary condition:

$$\frac{d\Pi}{dQ} = P + Q\frac{dP}{dQ} - \frac{dTC}{dQ} = 0 \tag{B.7}$$

if

$$\eta \equiv \frac{dQ}{dP} \cdot \frac{P}{Q} \text{ (price elasticity of demand)}$$

and

$$MC = \frac{dTC}{dQ} \text{ (marginal private costs)}$$

Then this necessary condition can be restated as follows:

$$P - MC = -\frac{QdP}{dQ} \tag{B.8}$$

and dividing both sides by P yields

$$\frac{P-MC}{P} = -\frac{QdP}{PdQ} = -\frac{1}{\eta} \tag{B.9}$$

This formulation is a version of the Lerner degree of monopoly expression.[a] It indicates the extent to which noncompetitive firms will mark up price relative to marginal private or firm costs. Note that in a perfectly competitive world the firm would be a price taker and "η" would be negative infinity. Thus $\frac{1}{\eta}$ is zero, and the positive pricing rule would be identical to the normative case, namely that $P = MC$, assuming that marginal private costs (MC) and marginal social costs ($g'(Q)$) were equal.

If marginal social costs are greater than marginal private costs as would be the case if negative externalities in the form of pollution are associated with each unit of output (Q) then the private profit maximizing price in a

[a]For a discussion of Lerner's markup equation, see S. Weintraub, *Intermediate Price Theory*, New York: Chilton Books, 1964.

competitive world would be less than the social welfare maximizing price and consumption would be excessive. Abstracting from such externalities as price elasticity increases from negative infinity (or being perfectly elastic) to become less elastic, the positive pricing rule shown in (9) would result in progressively greater markups over marginal private costs.

THE REVENUE CONSTRAINT

The Normative Case

With the positive and normative formulations described above it is possible to determine the implication of the public utility's revenue constraint. The normative development follows closely the work of Baumol and Bradford.[b] In order to initially simplify the formulation it will be assumed that the revenue constraint is set exogenously and does not depend upon output, (Q). Rather it is the amount of net income that a regulatory commission decides the firm should earn.

In order to make the development more applicable to current regulatory practices it will be assumed that there are n different customer types and each may have a different price elasticity of demand and the firm may have different costs in supplying these different customer types. Homogeneous demands and costs are assumed within each customer category.

Welfare will be defined under the present conditions in a manner analogous to the definition used previously. Total benefits are defined as the sum across customer types of the integral of the demand or marginal benefit function and total social costs are assumed to be equal to the sum of the total social costs of supplying each customer group. Therefore, the welfare function can be defined as:

$$W = \sum_{i=1}^{n} \int P_i dQ_i - \sum_{i=1}^{n} SC_i \qquad (B.10)$$

where

$P_i = f_i(Q_i)$ is the demand or willingness to pay function for the ith customer group, and

$SC_i = g_i(Q_i)$ is the social cost function of supplying the ith customer group

If it is assumed across customer groups that demands are independent and costs are fully separable then the regulatory constraint which fixes a revenue or income maximum can be analyzed by maximizing W subject to the following statement of the revenue constraint:

[b]W.J. Baumol, and D.F. Bradford, "Optimal Departures from Marginal Cost Pricing," *American Economic Review,* Vol. 60, June 1970.

$$TR = TC + R \tag{B.11}$$

where

$$TR = \text{total revenue} = \sum_{i=1}^{n} P_i Q_i$$

TC = total cost, which for simplicity can initially be assumed to be set equal to total social costs (SC)

$$\text{then } TC = \sum_{i=1}^{n} SC_i$$

R = allowed profits

The constrained objective function then becomes:

$$W^* = \sum_{i=1}^{n} \int P_i dQ_i - \sum_{i=1}^{n} SC_i$$

$$+ \lambda (\sum_{i=1}^{n} P_i Q_i - \sum_{i=1}^{n} SC_i - R) \tag{B.12}$$

Maximization of W^* yields the following set of necessary conditions:

$$\frac{\partial W^*}{\partial Q_i} = P_i - g_i'(Q_i) + \lambda(P_i + Q_i \frac{\partial P_i}{\partial Q_i} - g_i'(Q_i)) = 0 \tag{B.13}$$

for all $i = 1, n$

$$\frac{\partial W^*}{\partial \lambda} = \sum_{i=1}^{n} P_i Q_i - \sum_{i=1}^{n} SC_i - R = 0 \tag{B.14}$$

where

λ is the Lagrange multiplier and can be interpreted as the marginal welfare loss due to the regulatory constraint

If "$\eta_i \equiv \frac{\partial Q_i}{\partial P_i} \cdot \frac{P_i}{Q_i}$" is the price elasticity of demand for the ith group

and defined in a manner analogous to that used above, then the necessary condition for each ith group can be reformulated as follows:

$$(1+\lambda)(P_i - g_i'(Q_i)) = -\lambda Q_i \frac{\partial P_i}{\partial Q_i} \qquad \text{(B.14')}$$

Dividing by P_i yields:

$$(1+\lambda)\frac{(P_i - g_i'(Q_i))}{P_i} = -\lambda \frac{Q_i}{P_i}\frac{\partial P_i}{\partial Q_i} \qquad \text{(B.15)}$$

Rearranging terms further and substituting in "η_i" and MSC_i for $g_i'(Q_i)$ or the marginal social cost of supplying the ith customer group yields:

$$\frac{P_i - MSC_i}{P_i} = \frac{-\lambda}{1+\lambda}\frac{1}{\eta_i} \qquad \text{(B.15')}$$

The effect of the regulatory constraint on income is for the firm to deviate from marginal cost pricing. In a normative formulation such as this the objective function utilized requires that the loss in welfare is spread over each customer group in a manner that results in the least loss in total welfare for all groups taken collectively.

Two cases are important. A firm may earn too much revenue because costs are increasing and charging all customers their marginal cost may produce a surplus for the firm which exceeds R. Alternatively, costs may be decreasing, therefore charging all customers their marginal cost will fail to recover an income of R.

Note that the previous statement is a standard textbook summary. However, as Turvey points out, revenue constraints need not depend on the presence of increasing or decreasing costs to be important. He notes that:

> Marginal cost pricing, subject to any appropriate adjustments for nonoptimalities, may yield a revenue which provides a surplus in relation to accounting cost which is too high . . . or too low. . . . If this financial constraint is sacrosanct then some prices will have to be set below marginal costs (in the first case) or above (in the second). In either case a constraint which is effective will result in a welfare loss.[c]

Unless noted otherwise in what follows, an unambiguous mapping between the textbook and real world will be presumed. Increasing costs will be used to mean excess revenue and decreasing costs revenue shortfalls.

It is important to pursue the meaning of Equation (15') further for

---

[c] R. Turvey, *Optimal Pricing and Investment in Electricity Supply*, Cambridge, Massachusetts: The MIT Press, 1968, p. 89.

these two cases. It is also important to determine the appropriate range of λ for both the increasing cost excess revenue case and the decreasing cost revenue shortfall case. Consider Figure B-1. Under marginal cost pricing P_c and Q_c would be the price charged and quantity consumed by the ith customer group. If the resulting income is excessive then the regulatory constraint requires a lower price P_r and greater quantity Q_r. The shaded area in Figure B-1 represents this welfare loss. In order to understand the limits on λ it is useful to restate the discriminatory monopolist, perfectly competitive and regulatory pricing rules; where MSC_i and MC_i are identical.

Discriminating Monopolist: $\qquad \dfrac{P_i - MC_i}{P_i} = -\dfrac{1}{\eta_i}$

Competitive: $\qquad \dfrac{P_i - MC_i}{P_i} = 0, \therefore P_i = MC_i$

Regulatory: $\qquad \dfrac{P_i - MC_i}{P_i} = -\dfrac{\lambda}{1+\lambda} \dfrac{1}{\eta_i}$

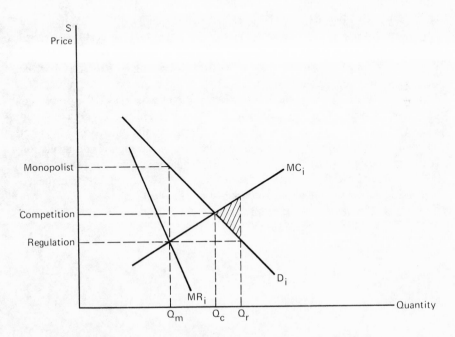

Figure B-1. Increasing Cost Case for ith Consumer Group

It should be noted from Figure B-1 that a discriminating monopolist will mark up price above marginal cost, while regulation would require prices to be set below marginal cost when marginal costs are increasing, therefore:

$$P_r < P_i < P_m \tag{B.16}$$

where

P_r = regulatory price

P_i = marginal cost price

P_m = discriminating monopolist price

From (B.16) and the previously stated pricing rules it follows that when marginal costs are increasing:

$$\frac{\lambda}{1+\lambda} < 0 < 1 \tag{B.16$'$}$$

$$-1 < \lambda < 0 \tag{B.16$''$}$$

Note that this means that when costs are increasing: (1) no customer should be charged a price which exceeds the marginal cost of supplying that customer, and (2) the percentage price decrease should be greatest for those customer groups which have the most *inelastic* demand.

The second case to consider is the decreasing cost case. This is the case that traditionally has been associated with many regulated industries. Different limits of λ and orderings of price are applicable under the decreasing cost case. Consider Figure B-2. When costs are decreasing, pricing based upon marginal cost will produce too little income. Under regulation, prices will be set above marginal cost but if the regulatory constraint is meaningful and regulation is effective in preventing the excesses of discriminatory pricing then these prices will be below those that a discriminatory monopolist would charge. The shaded area in Figure B-2 represents the welfare lost due to regulation.

The above pricing rules establish the following orderings of prices and λ for the decreasing cost case:

$$P_m > P_r > P_i \tag{B.17}$$

and, therefore:

$$1 > \frac{\lambda}{1+\lambda} > 0 \tag{B.17$'$}$$

and, if both inequalities hold then λ must be positive:

$$\therefore \qquad \lambda > 0 \qquad\qquad (B.17'')$$

Note $(17'')$ means that when costs are decreasing: (1) no customer should be charged a price which is less than the marginal cost of supplying him, and (2) the percentage price increase should be greatest for the most price inelastic group. However, if both constraints on "λ" are meaningful as an upper limit, the price markup for any customer group should be less under regulation than the price a perfectly discriminating monopolist would charge.

The Positive Case

There are several difficulties associated with developing a positive model for pricing with an exogenously set revenue constraint in a manner analogous to the previous comparison. The constraint utilized in (12) is mathematically identical to the profit maximizing objective function, when private and social costs are equal. In other words maximizing profit when profit is constrained to equal a fixed amount, R, is either trivial or underspecified.

To solve such problems there are at least two options. First, the profit maximizing objective function may be supplemented. For example, firms may be expected to minimize costs and to achieve the profit constraint, R, by

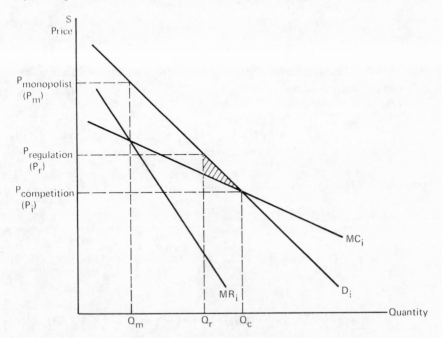

Figure B-2. Decreasing Cost Case for ith Consumer Group

producing the smallest possible output, Q. Additionally, restrictions that will lead to a single price for each category of use would further specify the problem and perhaps lead to a unique solution. Second, R may be treated as a ceiling rather than a specific amount. The problem could be treated as a nonlinear programing problem and the Kuhn-Tucker Theorem could be used to solve it. The problem could be formally stated as follows:

$$\Pi^* = \sum_{i=1}^{n} P_i Q_i - \sum_{i=1}^{n} g_i(Q_i) \tag{B.18}$$

$$\text{s.t.} \sum_{i=1}^{n} P_i Q_i - \sum_{i=1}^{n} g_i(Q_i) \leqslant R \tag{B.18a}$$

$$Q_i \geqslant 0 \tag{B.18b}$$

and (B.18a) may be rewritten as

$$\sum_{i=1}^{n} P_i Q_i - \sum_{i=1}^{n} g_i(Q_i) + s = R$$

where $s(\geqslant 0)$ is a slack variable. The optimization can now take place using a LaGrange approach, in which

$$Z = \Pi^* + \lambda(R - \sum_{i=1}^{n} P_i Q_i + \sum_{i=1}^{n} g_i(Q_i) - s) \tag{B.19}$$

is maximized. The first order conditions are:

$$i = 1, n$$

$$\frac{\partial Z}{\partial Q_i} = P_i + Q_i \frac{\partial P_i}{\partial Q_i} - g_i'(Q_i) + \lambda(-P_i - Q_i \frac{\partial P_i}{\partial Q_i} + g_i'(Q_i)) \leqslant 0 \tag{B.20}$$

$$\frac{\partial Z}{\partial Q_i} Q_i = (P_i + \frac{Q_i \partial P_i}{\partial Q_i} - g_i'(Q_i)) Q_i + \lambda(-P_i - Q_i \frac{\partial P_i}{\partial Q_i} + g_i'(Q_i)) Q_i = 0 \tag{B.20a}$$

$$Q_i \geqslant 0 \tag{B.20b}$$

$$\frac{\partial Z}{\partial \lambda} = R - \sum_{i=1}^{n} P_i Q_i + \sum_{i=1}^{n} g_i(Q_i) - s = 0 \tag{B.20c}$$

$$\frac{\partial Z}{\partial s} = -\lambda \leqslant 0 \tag{B.20d}$$

$$\frac{\partial Z}{\partial s} s = -\lambda s = 0 \tag{B.20e}$$

$$s \geqslant 0 \tag{B.20f}$$

Replacing s by $R - \sum_{i=1}^{n} P_i Q_i + \sum_{i=1}^{n} g_i(Q_i)$

yields the Kuhn-Tucker conditions which, when evaluated at P_i^*, Q_i^*, λ^* and s^* become:

$$i = 1, n$$

$$P_i^* + Q_i^* \frac{\partial P_i^*}{\partial Q_i^*} - g_i'(Q_i^*) + \lambda^*(-P_i^* - Q_i^* \frac{\partial P_i^*}{\partial Q_i^*} + g_i'(Q_i^*)) \leqslant 0 \tag{B.21}$$

$$P_i^* Q_i^* + Q_i \frac{\partial P_i^*}{\partial Q_i^*} Q_i^* - g_i'(Q_i^*) \cdot Q_i^* +$$

$$\lambda^*(-P_i^* Q_i^* - Q_i^* \frac{\partial P_i^*}{\partial Q_i^*} Q_i^* + g_i'(Q_i^*) Q_i^*) = 0 \tag{B.21a}$$

$$Q_i^* \geqslant 0 \tag{B.21b}$$

$$R - \sum_{i=1}^{n} P_i^* Q_i^* + \sum_{i=1}^{n} g_i(Q_i^*) \geqslant 0 \tag{B.21c}$$

$$\lambda^*(R - \Sigma P_i^* Q_i^* + \sum_{i=1}^{n} g_i(Q_i^*)) = 0 \tag{B.21d}$$

$$\lambda^* \geq 0 \qquad\qquad\qquad\qquad\qquad\qquad\qquad\qquad\text{(B.21e)}$$

Note that either $\lambda^* = 0$; or $R = \sum_{i=1}^{n} P_i^* Q_i^* - \sum_{i=1}^{n} g_i(Q_i^*)$; or both. In other words either the LaGrange multiplier vanishes or the inequality constraint is satisfied as a strict equality or both conditions hold. "While these conditions characterize a solution, it is certainly not apparent from them where the solution lies; that is, the Kuhn-Tucker conditions, while characterizing a solution, are in practice of little help in finding a solution."[d] These conditions can be related to the previous pricing rules for specific cases. For example, if λ^* equals zero and (21) is a strict equality, (this is necessary if $Q_i^* > 0$) the price markup equation will equal:

$$\frac{P_i^* - g_i'(Q_i^*)}{P_i^*} = -\frac{1}{\eta_i^*} \qquad\qquad\qquad\qquad\text{(B.21')}$$

And since g_i' *(Qi) equals MCi* (21') is identical to the Lerner markup equation of a nonregulated discriminating monopolist.

Note further that the set of terms in Equation (21) multiplied by λ^* is identical to the set of terms not multiplied by λ^*. This means that when λ^* does not equal zero it will equal either one or be indeterminate (0/0). This last result will occur, when each set of terms equals zero for all i categories. But this is the same way that a discriminating monopolist would price as indicated in (21'). Finally, it is important to note that when λ^* equals one, the set of terms multiplied by it does not have to sum to zero—in fact it may be less than or greater than zero in the "n" different separable markets of the regulated firm. In short the regulated firm may maximize its profits by pricing some of its "n" markets less than the monopoly level (marginal revenue equal marginal cost) and some above.

While a unique solution is not found in the Kuhn-Tucker conditions, it is important that regulators become aware of the potential for such inefficient pricing practices, if decisions are left solely to the regulated firms. Below we will consider some forms of regulation in which unique solutions and additional policy inferences are possible due to a restructuring of the profit constraint, but first peak and off peak pricing will be discussed.

PEAK LOAD PRICING

Economists have long seen value in a system of peak and off peak price differentials. In an important paper Oliver Williamson,[e] using a welfare function

---

[d]M. Intriligator, *Mathematical Optimization and Economic Theory*, Englewood Cliffs, N.J.: Prentice-Hall, 1971, pp. 54-55.

[e]O. Williamson, "Peak Load Pricing and Optimal Capacity Under Indivisibility Constraints," *American Economic Review*, LXI, Sept. 1966, pp. 810-27.

similar to that utilized above, determines optimal pricing rules when fixed or capacity costs and variable or operating costs vary at peak and off peak times. It is a straightforward task to extend the previously determined pricing rules to this case.

Let there be only two time periods, which we will define as on peak (p) and off peak (o). Further, let there be only two customer groups, 1 and 2 and assume that customer 1 consumes only off peak and customer 2 only on peak. The appropriate objective function can be stated as follows:

$$W = \int P_1 dQ_1 + \int P_2 dQ_2 - C_o - C_p \tag{B.22}$$

where

$\int P_i dQ_i$ are the respective areas under the demand schedules

C_o is the off peak variable cost and a function of $Q \, (= h \, (Q_1))$

C_p is the on peak cost and has two components: C_p^o is the variable or operating cost during peak periods ($= g(Q_2)$) and C_p^k is the annual capacity cost that is incurred in order to maintain sufficient capacity to supply peak period demands ($= k(Q_2)$).

Maximizing W yields the following set of necessary conditions:

$$\frac{\partial W}{\partial Q_1} = P_1 - h'(Q_1) = 0 \tag{B.23}$$

$$\frac{\partial W}{\partial Q_2} = P_2 - g'(Q_2) - k'(Q_2) = 0 \tag{B.23'}$$

where

$h'(Q_1)$ is the marginal operating cost of supplying off peak

$g'(Q_2)$ is the marginal operating costs on peak

$k'(Q_2)$ is the marginal capacity costs annualized to on peak use

$$P_1 = h'(Q_1) \tag{B.24}$$

$$P_2 = g'(Q_2) + k'(Q_2) \tag{B.24'}$$

Equations (24) and (24') may be readily generalized. Williamson defines capacity costs on the basis of the amount of time over a year that any customer utilizes capacity and the percent of time that capacity is fully utilized. It is simpler to consider the on peak and off peak as two separate services and to define off peak costs only in terms of operating costs and on peak costs in terms of both operating and annual capacity costs. If demands are independent then a separate demand schedule can be established for each customer group for on peak and off peak use. In the case of electricity this would mean that prices off peak would be set equal to marginal operating or energy costs and prices on peak would be equal to the marginal operating (energy) plus the marginal capacity costs.

By defining peak as those periods of time over which the last unit of installed capacity would be necessary it is unnecessary to worry about weights for percentage of usage. Instead, on peak prices can be established and recovered from all who use the system during peak periods. In its more general form the welfare function is as follows:

$$W = \sum_{i=1}^{n} \int P_i^o dQ_i^o + \sum_{i=1}^{n} \int P_i^p dQ_i^p - \sum_{i=1}^{n} SC_i^o - \sum_{i=1}^{n} SC_i^p \qquad (B.25)$$

where

P_i^o, Q_i^o, and SC_i^o are the off peak prices, quantities, and costs for the ith customer, and

P_i^p, Q_i^p, and SC_i^p are the on peak prices, quantities, and costs for the ith customer.

Maximizing (B.25) yields the following necessary conditions:

$$P_i^o = MC_i^o = \text{Marginal Energy Costs off peak} \qquad (B.26)$$

all $i = 1, n$

$$P_i^p = MC_i^p = \text{Marginal Energy Costs on peak plus Marginal Capacity Costs}$$

all $i = 1, n$

If the assumption of demand independence is continued it is a straightforward step to add the regulatory constraint utilized above. The new objective function becomes:

$$W^* = \sum_{i=1}^{n} \int P_i^o dQ_i^o + \sum_{i=1}^{n} \int P_i^p dQ_i^p - \sum_{i=1}^{n} SC_i^o - \sum_{i=1}^{n} SC_i^p$$

$$+ \lambda (\sum_{i=1}^{n} (P_i^o Q_i^o - SC_i^o) + \sum_{i=1}^{n} (P_i^p Q_i^p - SC_i^p) - R) \qquad (B.27)$$

Maximizing (B.27) yields the following set of necessary conditions:

$$\frac{\partial W^*}{\partial Q_i^O} = P_i^O - MC_i^O + \lambda(P_i^O + Q_i^O \frac{\partial P_i^O}{\partial Q_i^O} - MC_i^O) = 0 \qquad \text{(B.28)}$$

all $i = 1, n$

$$\frac{\partial W^*}{\partial Q_i^p} = P_i^p - MC_i^p + \lambda(P_i^p - Q_i^p \frac{\partial P_i^p}{\partial Q_i^p} - MC_i^p) = 0 \qquad \text{(B.28')}$$

all $i = 1, n$

$$\frac{\partial W^*}{\partial \lambda} = \sum_{i=1}^{n} (P_i^O Q_i^O - SC_i^O) + \sum_{i=1}^{n} (P_i^p Q_i^p - SC_i^p) - R = 0 \qquad \text{(B.28'')}$$

Solving (B.28) and (B.28') yields the following pricing rules:

$$\frac{P_i^O - MC_i^O}{P_i^O} = -\frac{\lambda}{1+\lambda} \frac{1}{\eta_i^O} \qquad \text{(B.29)}$$

$$\frac{P_i^p - MEC_i^p - MCC_i^p}{P_i^p} = -\frac{\lambda}{1+\lambda} \frac{1}{\eta_i^p} \qquad \text{(B.29')}$$

where

MC_i^O is the marginal off peak costs (energy cost)

MEC_i^p is the marginal energy cost on peak

MCC_i^p is the marginal capacity cost on peak (note each marginal cost is presumed to be measured in identical units)

η_i^O is the price elasticity of demand off peak = $(\frac{\partial Q_i^O}{\partial P_i^O} \cdot \frac{P_i^O}{Q_i^O})$

η_i^p is the price elasticity of demand on peak = $(\frac{\partial Q_i^p}{\partial P_i^p} \cdot \frac{P_i^p}{Q_i^p})$

Note the independence assumption means that $\dfrac{\partial Q_i^o}{\partial P_i^p} = 0$ and $\dfrac{\partial Q_i^p}{\partial P_i^o} = 0$.

In short, peak load pricing rules merely convert the normative pricing rules of marginal cost and regulation to a more finely distinguished form. Short run marginal cost pricing off peak, plus short run and allowances for capacity incremental costs on peak, are substituted for marginal costs. The number of periods may be extended beyond two if operating or energy costs off peak are variable at different off peak times.

When positive profit maximizing models are considered, an additional way to price discriminate is established. If the demand independent assumption is maintained the positive pricing rules that result are identical to those established above. Prices are marked above the appropriate on peak or off peak marginal costs inversely proportional to the corresponding price elasticity of demand. Two qualifications should be noted.

In two important recent papers Bailey points out that profit maximizing regulated firms may deviate from the normative welfare maximizing pricing rules shown above in (29) and (29′). Regulated firms may seek capital investment, Bailey points out, "Because constrained profits increase with the level of capacity, the firm passes on the benefits of regulation to those users whose increased demand will cause an increase in capacity."[f] This means that there may be a tendency to overprice off peak use and underprice on peak use for regulated firms. In a further paper[g] Bailey and White also point out that when differences in price elasticities of demand are considered it is even theoretically possible for on peak prices to fall below off peak prices "for a profit maximizing firm subject to a regulatory constraint on its rate of return."

Additionally, the costs of meeting on peak and off peak service may not be independent. An electric utility might design new capacity for peak in a way that takes into account the system's off peak operating cost. If such cost interdependencies are present the joint product, firm (positive) and a social welfare maximizer (normative) would take these into account in establishing prices. Weintraub[h] considers the positive case and concludes that prices or marginal revenue should be set equal to the goods own marginal cost plus (or minus) any negative (or positive) effects the expansion of the good's output has on the other goods produced by the firm.

If, for example, actual on peak costs were higher under one particular system design than under an alternative design, but the second was selected, since it had lower operating costs off peak, then it would be

---

[f]E. Bailey, "Peak-Load Pricing Under Regulatory Constraint," *Journal of Political Economy*, Vol. 80 (July/August), 1972, p. 675.

[g]E. Bailey and L.J. White, "Reversals in Peak and Off Peak Prices," *The Bell Journal of Economics and Management Science*, forthcoming.

[h]S. Weintraub, *Intermediate Price Theory*, New York: Chilton Books, 1964, Chapter 15.

appropriate to take such cost interdependencies into account in pricing on and off peak electricity. The former would be reduced and the latter increased relative to their respective marginal costs. Under such conditions the range in which the appropriate on peak price falls would be between the ceiling of the actual on peak costs and the costs on peak if there were no other services provided by the firm. It must be emphasized, however, that such deviations from strict marginal cost pricing are due to cost interdependencies and should not be implemented, as it is sometimes averred, for reasons of fairness or equity in the treatment of on and off peak uses.[i]

RELAXING THE DEMAND INDEPENDENCE ASSUMPTION

It is important to analyze the effect of relaxing the assumption of independence across demands for two reasons. First, the expectation of peak and off peak price differentials is that this will cause a substitution of the latter for the former. Second, in a positive (i.e., profit maximizing) decision maker's world the incentive to price discriminate in various markets would, a priori, appear to be different from a normative (i.e., welfare maximization) world.

In order to keep the mathematics simple it will be assumed that there are two markets, which may be distinguished based upon time of day or customer category differences. The quantity demanded in each depends upon its own price and the price in the other market. Costs are assumed to be independent. Therefore,

$$P_1 = f(Q_1, P_2) \qquad\qquad (B.30)$$

$$P_2 = g(Q_2, P_1)$$

If these alternative specifications of the willingness to pay or demand functions are substituted in the welfare functions used above, (12) or (22), the necessary conditions for welfare maximization can be derived by maximizing W^{**}; note the equality between social and private costs continues to be presumed:

$$W^{**} = \sum_{i=1}^{2} \int P_i dQ_i - \sum_{i=1}^{2} SC_i + \lambda \left(\sum_{i=1}^{2} P_i Q_i - \sum_{i=1}^{2} SC_i - R \right)$$

$$= \int f(Q_1, P_2) dQ_1 + \int g(Q_2, P_1) dQ_2 - \sum_{i=1}^{2} SC_i$$

---

[i]For a further discussion of this point see Turvey's discussion of the difference between "ceteris paribus marginal cost" and "mutatis mutandis marginal cost" pricing for electric utilities, see page 78 in R. Turvey, *Economic Analysis and Public Enterprises*, Totowa, N.J.: Rowman and Littlefield, 1971.

$$+ \lambda(f(Q_1,P_2)Q_1 + g(Q_2,P_1)Q_2 - \overset{2}{\underset{i=1}{\Sigma}} SC_i - R) \qquad (B.31)$$

Maximizing (B.31) yields the following set of necessary conditions:

$$\frac{\partial W^{**}}{\partial Q_1} = P_1 - MC_1 + \lambda(P_1 + Q_1 \frac{\partial P_1}{\partial Q_1} + Q_2 \frac{\partial P_2}{\partial Q_1} - MC_1) = 0 \quad (B.32a)$$

$$\frac{\partial W^{**}}{\partial Q_2} = P_2 - MC_2 + \lambda(P_2 + Q_2 \frac{\partial P_2}{\partial Q_2} + Q_1 \frac{\partial P_1}{\partial Q_2} - MC_2) = 0 \quad (B.32b)$$

$$\frac{\partial W^{**}}{\partial \lambda} = P_1 f(P_1,P_2) + P_2 g(P_1,P_2) - SC_1 - SC_2 - R = 0 \quad (B.33)$$

Solving (B.32a) yields a price markup equation analogous to those considered above.

$$(1+\lambda)(P_1 - MC_1) = -\lambda(Q_1 \frac{\partial P_1}{\partial Q_1} + Q_2 \frac{\partial P_2}{\partial Q_1}) \qquad (B.32a')$$

Dividing by P_1 yields:

$$\frac{P_1 - MC_1}{P_1} = -\frac{\lambda}{(1+\lambda)} (\frac{Q_1 \partial P_1}{P_1 \partial Q_1} + \frac{Q_2}{P_1} \frac{\partial P_2}{\partial Q_1} 0) \qquad (B.34)$$

The first term in brackets on the right hand side is the inverse of the price elasticity. The second term does not have a familiar economic interpretation. In general $(\frac{\partial Q_1}{\partial P_2} \neq \frac{\partial Q_2}{\partial P_1})$; however under certain conditions they may be equal. Consider the pair of Slutsky equations involved for a single consumer:

$$\frac{\partial Q_1}{\partial P_2} = \left[\frac{\partial Q_1}{\partial P_2}\right]_{\text{utility constant}} - Q_2 \left[\frac{\partial Q_1}{\partial Y}\right]_{\text{prices constant}} \quad (B.35)$$

$$\frac{\partial Q_2}{\partial P_1} = \left[\frac{\partial Q_2}{\partial P_1}\right]_{\text{utility constant}} - Q_1 \left[\frac{\partial Q_2}{\partial Y}\right]_{\text{prices constant}} \quad (B.36)$$

The first terms on the right hand side of Equations (35) and (36) will always be equal. When the second terms (income effects) are negligible, as they will be when Q_1 and Q_2 make up a small part of the budget, then conditions will be such that the so-called symmetry conditions hold.

$$\frac{\partial Q_1}{\partial P_2} = \frac{\partial Q_2}{\partial P_1} \tag{B.37}$$

Substituting (B.37) in (B.34) yields a more familiar set of economic expressions:

$$\frac{P_1 - MC_1}{P_1} = - \frac{\lambda}{1+\lambda} \left(\frac{1}{\eta_1} + \frac{Q_2}{P_1} \cdot \frac{\partial P_1}{\partial Q_2} \right) \tag{B.34'}$$

$$\frac{P_1 - MC_1}{P_1} = - \frac{\lambda}{1+\lambda} \left(\frac{1}{\eta_1} + \frac{1}{\epsilon_{21}} \right) \tag{B.34''}$$

where

ϵ_{21} is the cross elasticity of the demand for 2 with respect to the price of 1.

Similarly, the price markup for 2 may be written as:

$$\frac{P_2 - MC_2}{P_2} = - \frac{\lambda}{1+\lambda} \left(\frac{1}{\eta_2} + \frac{1}{\epsilon_{12}} \right) \tag{B.38}$$

Note that if (1) and (2) are rival goods, ϵ_{ij} will be positive. Therefore, it will tend to offset the effect of η_i which is negative. If costs were increasing, price decreases would be in order but the percentage price decrease would be smaller if interdependent demands were taken into account, since any relative price change that merely shifts use to the other market will not necessarily avoid the excess output inefficiencies of regulation. Similarly, if costs are decreasing the price markups would also be less if markets were interdependent. Furthermore, in the latter case the ratio of $\dfrac{\lambda}{1+\lambda}$ is between 0 and 1 and this further mitigates deviations in prices from marginal costs in the normative world.

Rees[j] considers a similar objective function and case. The mathematical conclusions are identical; however, Rees prefers to consider a complementary relationship as one in which revenues are increased from the second good when the price of the joint product under consideration is raised. Of course, under the present conditions, this would occur when the two joint products were competitive. An additional factor must be noted when (34'') and Rees's results are considered. Both derivations are special cases, since they explain the pricing behavior of firms when the price of one joint product is being established but the price of the firm's other joint products are taken as given.

[j]R. Rees, "Second Best Pricing Rules for Public Enterprise Pricing," *Economica*, August 1968.

In a more general case, the prices of both will be established jointly. In a recent paper by Smith, Cicchetti, and Gillen[k] and testimony by Baumol[l] this general case is considered. Their conclusion is that in both a normative and positive world, prices should be established by taking into account the price elasticity of each interdependent product, as well as the various cross-elasticity effects.

Finally, although the above extensions were developed for only two interdependent markets it is easy to generalize to n markets if the symmetry conditions hold. Note that the symmetry conditions discussed above are not easily interpreted when markets are distinguished by customer category as opposed to time-of-day price differentials. Indeed the Slutsky equations referred to above are relevant for individual, but not for aggregate demands that are distinguished by broad categories, such as residential, commercial, and industrial. However, customer category demands are far more likely to be independent than time-of-day markets for the same customer.

In addition, the notion that a residential demander will react to a price increase in the commercial market the same way that a commercial demander will react to a price increase in the residential market seems to stretch the notion referred to above as "symmetry conditions" beyond the bounds dictated by expositional expediency. Accordingly, the policy significance of the above results for peak-off peak pricing is far more important than discrimination in interdependent categories of customer markets. Finally, another type of interdependence in demand, which is likely to be important in practice, is any intertemporal interdependence for a particular customer in different time periods. Smith, Cicchetti, and Gillen refer to this special case in detail in their Amos Tuck paper.

AVERCH-JOHNSON OUTPUT BIAS

Previously a regulatory constraint was considered when revenue requirements (R) were set exogenously. A considerable literature has grown out of the work of Averch-Johnson[m] and Wellisz.[n] Much of the literature has dealt with the effect of rate base regulation on input hiring distortions. It is probably at least as important to consider the impact of rate base regulation on prices and output levels. Up to this point the amount of income that a regulated firm was

[k]V.K. Smith, C.J. Cicchetti, and W.J. Gillen, "Electric Power Regulation Externalities and the A-J-W Effect," presented at Seminar on Problems of Regulation and Public Utilities, The Amos Tuck School of Business Administration, Dartmouth College, August 1973.

[l]W.J. Baumol, "Pricing for Allocative Efficiency with Non-Zero Cross Elasticity," Bell Exhibit 26B, FCC Docket No. 16258, February 14, 1968.

[m]H. Averch and L.L. Johnson, "Behavior of the Firm Under Regulatory Constraints," *American Economic Review*, Vol. 52, 1962.

[n]S.H. Wellisz, "Regulation of Natural Gas Pipeline Companies: An Economic Analysis," *Journal of Political Economy*, February 1963, pp. 30-43.

permitted to earn above total costs (R) was assumed to be set exogenously. It is probably more accurate to view current regulation as setting an acceptable rate of return "r", which may be earned in income above the annual costs of the current rate base and operating costs.

If "R" or the income that can be earned is determined on the basis of rate base then this may be stated as:

$$R = (K^* - AD)r \tag{B.34}$$

where

ρ = fair rate of return

r = fair rate of return minus the cost of capital (p_k)

K^* = total capital investment

AD = depreciation of past investment

By substituting Equation (34) into the previously utilized welfare functions and adding an additional constraint to take into account the fact that output (Q_i) depends upon capital $(K = (K^*-AD))$ and labor (L) the constrained welfare function becomes:

$$W^{**} = \sum_{i=1}^{n} \int P_i dQ_i \qquad - \sum_{i=1}^{n} g_i(Q_i) \tag{B.40}$$

$$+ \lambda(\sum_{i=1}^{n} P_i Q_i \qquad - \sum_{i=1}^{n} g_i(Q_i) - rK)$$

$$+ (\sum_{i=1}^{n} \mu_i(Q_i - F_i(K,L)))$$

where

μ_i is the LaGrange multiplier for the production function constraints

$g_i(Q_i) = wL_i + p_k K_i$

w is the unit wage rate

L is the amount of labor employed $(= \sum_{i=1}^{n} L_i)$

p_k is the unit price of capital

$$K = \sum_{i=1}^{n} K_i$$

$$r = \rho - p_k$$

Note that the total social cost will be presumed to equal total private costs $(wL + p_k K)$, and $g_i'(Q_i) = MC_i$; therefore, maximizing (40) yields:

$$\frac{\partial W^{***}}{\partial Q_i} = P_i - MC_i + \lambda(P_i + Q_i \frac{\partial P_i}{\partial Q_i} - MC_i) + \mu_i(1) = 0 \qquad (B.41)$$

all $i = 1, n$

$$\frac{\partial W^{***}}{\partial K_i} = -r\lambda + \mu_i(-\frac{\partial Q_i}{\partial K_i}) = 0 \qquad (B.42)$$

all $i = 1, n$

$$\therefore \mu_i = \frac{r\lambda}{-\dfrac{\partial Q_i}{\partial K_i}} \qquad (B.42')$$

and the marginal physical product of capital in the production of Q_i is defined as $MPP_{Ki} = \dfrac{\partial Q_i}{\partial K_i}$. Therefore:

$$-\mu_i = \frac{r\lambda}{MPP_{Ki}} \qquad (B.42'')$$

Substituting (B.42'') into (B.41) yields the following expression:

$$P_i - MC_i + \lambda(P_i + Q_i \frac{\partial P_i}{\partial Q_i} - MC_i) - \frac{r\lambda}{MPP_{Ki}} = 0 \qquad (B.43)$$

Solving for the price markup term yields:

$$(1+\lambda)(P_i - MC_i) = -\lambda(Q_i \frac{\partial P_i}{\partial Q_i} - \frac{r}{MPP_{Ki}}) \qquad (B.43')$$

$$(P_i - MC_i) = \frac{-\lambda}{1+\lambda}\ (Q_i \frac{\partial P_i}{\partial Q_i} - \frac{r}{MPP_{Ki}}) \qquad (\text{B.43}'')$$

Rearranging terms and dividing both sides by P_i yields the following expression:

$$\frac{P_i - MC_i}{P_i} = -\frac{\lambda}{1+\lambda}\ (\frac{Q_i}{P_i}\frac{\partial P_i}{\partial Q_i} - \frac{r}{P_i MPP_{Ki}}) \qquad (\text{B.44})$$

$$= -\frac{\lambda}{1+\lambda}\ (\frac{1}{\eta_i} - \frac{r}{MVP_{Ki}})$$

where

MVP_{Ki} is the marginal value product of capital in the production of $Q_i (= P_i MPP_{Ki})$.

Equation (B.44) may be rewritten in order to contrast it with the fixed financial revenue constraint derived in Equation (B.15′) above:

$$\frac{P_i - MC_i - \frac{\lambda}{1+\lambda}\frac{r}{MPP_{Ki}}}{P_i} = \frac{-\lambda}{1+\lambda}\ (\frac{1}{\eta_i}) \qquad (\text{B.44}')$$

There are three factors that are important for any policy discussion of (44) and (44′). First, as with previous cases excess revenue implies price decreases or markdowns; while revenue deficits imply price markups. The term $(-\lambda/1+\lambda)$ is, therefore, positive when revenue excesses and/or price markdowns are necessary and negative when revenue deficits and/or price markups are necessary.

There is an important distinction between this endogenous revenue constraint and the fixed or exogenously set revenue constraint considered above. In the latter case revenue excesses or shortfalls may be dealt with by a single policy variable, namely decreasing or increasing prices. In the present case the amount of net revenue that can be earned by the firm is variable, furthermore it depends on the amount of capital the firm has invested. Accordingly, the regulatory constraint can be met in two ways by adjusting price levels and by expanding or contracting the amount of capital the firm has invested. The additional term on the right hand side of (44) reflects this difference.

If the fair rate of return (ρ) exceeds the price of capital (p_k), $r/P_i MPP_{Ki}$ will be positive. Further, as the amount of additional capital required (∂K_i) to increase output (∂Q_i) increases the additional term in (44) will increase in significance. In several cases this adjustment will not matter. First, off peak service requires very little, if any, additional capital to be supplied. For such cases the adjustment term vanishes and the two forms of regulatory constraint have the same pricing rule. When the fair return and price of capital are equal, the two forms of regulatory constraint also reduce to equivalent statements about price deviations from marginal cost.

The two forms of the regulatory constraint may differ, and it is important to understand why. If firms are marking down prices because they have excess revenue, the inverse price elasticity rule suggests that the more inelastic demanders should have the largest percentage price decrease from marginal cost. The revised rule found in (44) would amend this by suggesting that, if a user was expected to increase use that would require an increase in capital, then the amount of net revenue that could be earned would be increased.

From a welfare maximizing standpoint the adjustment to the price markup equation may make it possible to come closer to marginal cost pricing, thus increasing social welfare. To understand the conditions under which this result will take place, note that the allowed net income was previously considered to be a constant (R) and therefore independent of output (Q). Under the regulatory constraint considered in this section the allowed net income is dependent upon Q, since it equals ($\rho - p_k)K$ and $Q = F(K,L)$. Additionally, the marginal physical product of capital is non negative (i.e., $\frac{\partial Q}{\partial K} \geqslant 0$); therefore, as Q expands the allowed net income will increase if the marginal physical product is positive. When it is zero the two regulatory constraints will be equivalent. But when prices are marked down from marginal costs the firm will expand output, and if capital also increases it will be permitted to earn more net income, thus requiring less additional markdowns and therefore less deviation from marginal cost pricing and greater social welfare.

The opposite situation holds when prices are marked up. Volume is reduced and capital requirements (and therefore allowed net income) may decline. But when a firm marks up its price from marginal cost it causes a loss of welfare. Since the amount of markup depends upon the size of the net revenue shortfall, the variable net revenue constraint—which in this case declines in magnitude—will once again lead to less deviation from marginal cost pricing.

Therefore, welfare losses will be less than when the revenue constraint is fixed and independent of output, Q.

In practice the fixed (R) may be viewed as a short run form of regulation in which adjustments for output and therefore investment are not possible. The variable regulatory constraint $((\rho - p_k)K)$ permits greater flexibility. Therefore when it is contrasted with the more inflexible rule set at the same initial level of net allowable income, it requires less deviation from marginal cost pricing and therefore less loss in social welfare.

Normative considerations of A-J bias are a useful benchmark to ascertain the manner in which welfare maximization would attempt to minimize the inefficiencies of deviations from marginal cost pricing and a regulatory process which itself may also increase costs. However, the predominant interest in A-J bias has been associated with the positive impact of this form of regulation on the firm. Therefore, it is important to develop the parallel pricing rule for the firm under such rate base regulation.

Imposing the same form of rate base regulation constraints in the profit maximizing objective function yields the following constrained objective function:

$$\Pi^{***} = \sum_{i=1}^{n} P_i Q_i - \sum_{i=1}^{n} g_i(Q_i) + \lambda \left(\sum_{i=1}^{n} P_i Q_i - \sum_{i=1}^{n} g_i(Q_i) - rK \right)$$

$$= \left(\sum_{i=1}^{n} \mu_i (Q_i - F_i(K,L)) \right) \tag{B.45}$$

where $\qquad K = \sum_{i=1}^{n} K_i$

$g_i(Q_i)$ is the least cost way of producing output $Q_i = wL_i + p_k K_i$. Maximizing (45) yields the following subset of necessary conditions, when $MC_i = g_i'(Q_i)$.

$$\frac{\partial \Pi^{***}}{\partial Q_i} = P_i + Q_i \frac{\partial P_i}{\partial Q_i} - MC_i + \lambda (P_i + Q_i \frac{\partial P_i}{\partial Q_i} - MC_i) + \mu_i = 0 \tag{B.46}$$

all $i = 1, n$

$$\frac{\partial \Pi^{***}}{\partial K_i} = -r\lambda + \mu_i (- \frac{\partial Q_i}{\partial K_i}) = 0 \tag{B.47}$$

$$\therefore \ \mu_i = - \frac{r\lambda}{\dfrac{\partial Q_i}{\partial K_i}} \tag{B.47'}$$

Substituting (B.47') into (B.46) yields the following derivation of the price markup equation:

$$(1+\lambda)(P_i - MC_i) = -(1+\lambda)(Q_i \frac{\partial P_i}{\partial Q_i}) + \frac{\lambda r}{\dfrac{\partial Q_i}{\partial K_i}} \tag{B.48}$$

Dividing by P_i and $(1+\lambda)$ yields:

$$\frac{P_i - MC_i}{P_i} = -\frac{1}{\eta_i} + (\frac{\lambda}{1+\lambda}) \frac{r}{P_i \dfrac{\partial Q_i}{\partial K_i}} \tag{B.49}$$

$$= -\frac{1}{\eta_i} + (\frac{\lambda}{1+\lambda}) \frac{r}{MVP_{Ki}} \tag{B.49'}$$

Under the positive theory of regulatory models, it is usually assumed that profit maximization would lead firms to earn excess revenues over cost. The regulatory constraint is usually thought to hold prices below the monopoly level. In the A-J-W model derived above a second feature, namely non least cost production, is also possible. Equation (49') makes it possible to analyze the types of tradeoffs that would be followed by an all-knowing profit maximizing firm subject to a revenue constraint that depends upon the level of capital investment.

Two straightforward cases should be noted at the outset. First, if regulation is not binding then λ will be zero and the firm will attempt to behave like a perfectly discriminating monopolist as previously derived above in Equation (9). Second, a similar conclusion can be drawn when the cost of capital (p_k) and fair rate of return (ρ) are equal.

The more subtle conclusions can be drawn from noting that when regulation is binding it will normally be expected to lead to price markups (downs) which are less (greater) than the discriminating monopolists. Excess revenue from a regulatory perspective will, therefore, lead one to expect a negative sign for the term $\frac{\lambda}{1+\lambda}$, since $r(=\rho - p_k)$ and $\frac{\partial Q_i}{\partial K_i}$ are usually presumed to be greater than or equal to zero. The negative term $\frac{\lambda}{1+\lambda}$ implies that regulation will not permit firms to price at levels as high as discriminating monopolists.

Several interesting cases are shown in Table B-1. The combination of small price elasticity and non capital intensiveness (a large marginal physical product of capital, $\frac{\partial Q_i}{\partial K_i}$) will lead to the greatest markup of price over marginal cost. The least price markup occurs in the more price elastic most capital intensive case.

These results were hinted at above when Bailey's important work was referenced.[o] The intermediate cases indicate profit maximizing firms face a pricing tradeoff when confronting customers with differing elasticities and capital intensiveness. The term "capital intensiveness" is one of those antiseptic phrases used by economists. However, it should be noted that on peak service has, by definition, a smaller marginal physical product of capital than off peak service. From a policy standpoint this means that profit maximizing decision makers will attempt to increase off peak prices by more than on peak prices and when elasticity enters, the most inelastic off peak customers are those that will have the highest price markups relative to marginal costs.

_____
[o]For a far more complete discussion of pricing behavior under peak load pricing and various objective functions see Bailey, op. cit., and Bailey and White, op. cit.

Table B-1. Pricing Behavior of Profit Maximizing Rate Base Regulated Firms

Assume: fair rate of return exceeds price of capital; regulation is binding in holding prices below discriminating monopoly levels

Marginal Physical Product of Capital	Price Markups	
	Price Elastic	Price Inelastic
Small	Least	Intermediate
Large	Intermediate	Greatest

SUMMARY

In the previous discussion it was concluded that marginal cost pricing was the starting point of any normative pricing rule. When marginal social costs exceed marginal private costs, as they would when negative externalities vary with output, an upward adjustment in prices is necessary. When costs differ at different times of day or in different markets then the relevant time of day or market based marginal cost should be the basis for setting prices.

Regulation creates economic inefficiencies. When marginal costs are decreasing extra revenue must be collected to make the firm whole. Pricing inelastic uses more, relative to their marginal costs, than price elastic uses will lead to a minimization of the welfare loss associated with regulatory inefficiency. Regulated firms, which are more likely to be concerned with profit maximization than welfare maximization, would tend to move beyond the pricing patterns of welfare maximization and attempt to achieve the profit goals of a discriminating monopolist.

Regulation may cause inefficiency through higher costs and input distortions; we noted that welfare maximization requires the setting of prices to minimize such inefficiencies. However, additional incentives to deviate from marginal cost pricing may be imposed on the regulated, profit maximizing firm under rate base regulation. Accordingly, although normative and positive pricing rules may sometimes lead to adjustments in price in the same direction, regulatory commissions must guard against any tendency to exceed the normative welfare maximizing limits. The simplest guide is to require that all uses will either have a price markup in decreasing cost cases and a price markdown in increasing cost cases. Commissions should not permit positive behavior to raise some prices above costs and lower others. Finally, regulatory commissions should come to realize that any regulated firm's tendency to price in this way is a direct consequence of both regulation and the way it is implemented.

POSTSCRIPT: BLOCK PRICING
AND REGULATED FIRMS

Throughout the entire previous discussion, positive and normative pricing rules were established for a number of different situations that may more or less be expected to be relevant for regulated firms. In *all* cases the pricing rules so derived restricted the price schedules to flat tariffs. That is, notwithstanding the fact that prices could differ for different categories of customers on the basis of either cost or demand differences or both, within each separately defined submarket a single price was derived for both marginal and inframarginal use.

Frequently this has meant that the regulatory constraint requires the acceptance of pricing in an inefficient manner. When costs are decreasing prices are marked up for all but more for the inelastic demanders and vice versa for the increasing cost case. One way to avoid such inefficiencies would be to price the outputs of a regulated firm in such a way that all marginal use is priced at marginal cost and revenue shortfalls (excesses) are made up from (returned to) inframarginal use.

While such a plan would mean one or more declining blocks when costs are decreasing (and one or more increasing blocks when costs were increasing), it is absolutely essential, in order to make unambiguous statements about social welfare maximization, that such a pattern of block pricing does not affect any marginal consumption decisions. The informational requirements are far greater—and, in addition, the regulatory enforcement problems are much more pronounced—than the flat rate inverse price elasticity rules described above.

The reason for greater regulatory problems is that if firms are permitted to collect extra revenue in early blocks by charging prices in excess of marginal costs, then this extra revenue could be used to drop the prices of some higher use blocks below marginal costs. Several simple rules will aid regulators to guard against such positive world excesses: (1) no tail block prices should be allowed to deviate from marginal cost; (2) at a minimum, a considerable number of users in a given consumer category should be consuming in the tail block; and (3) if costs are increasing rising blocks should be utilized. If costs are constant, block pricing is not appropriate; if costs are decreasing, declining blocks should be utilized.

Despite the above qualifications, the informational needs to appropriately establish cost and demand based on block pricing (along with the regulatory enforcement problems associated with it) are such that the single flat price is preferable in practice. Furthermore, if peak-off peak pricing is viewed as an ultimate pricing system, varying block pricing is inconsistent with this objective.

Appendix C

Other Federal Power
Agencies

BONNEVILLE POWER ADMINISTRATION

The Bonneville Power Administration (BPA) is responsible for the marketing of electric power produced at 33 federal dams built and operated either by the U.S. Army Corps of Engineers or the Bureau of Reclamation. It serves the area drained by the Columbia River including the states of Washington, Oregon, Idaho, Montana (west of the Continental Divide), and small adjacent portions of California, Nevada, Utah, and Wyoming. BPA supplies about 55 percent of the power generated in the region and has the capacity to transmit about 80 percent of the region's power.

In addition to coordinating the development of the Columbia River with Canadian authorities in an effort to maximize flood control and generation potential, BPA is a signatory to a long term coordination agreement between the federal government and fourteen of the region's public and private utilities. BPA also participates in a regional hydro-thermal program designed to build and operate large thermal plants to meet regional base load needs. BPA will provide most of the high voltage bulk transmission, hydroelectric peaking capacity, and reserves.

In further cooperation with private and public utilities BPA has participated in the construction and operation of the Pacific Northwest-Pacific Southwest extra high voltage transmission intertie that links the Federal Columbia River Power System with Los Angeles. Surplus secondary energy and peaking capacity is sold to the Pacific Southwest, while the Pacific Northwest is expected to receive off peak steam energy during periods of low stream flow. Finally, under wheeling agreements between BPA and nonfederal utilities, power from nonfederal plants is wheeled (transported) over the BPA transmission grid.

The Administrator of BPA is appointed by and responsible to the Secretary of the Interior, and is authorized to build a transmission grid "in order

157

to encourage the widest possible use of all electric energy that can be generated and marketed and to provide reasonable outlets therefor, and to prevent the monopolization thereof by limited groups" (16 USC 832a(b)).

By explicit statutory declaration Bonneville generation is to "be operated for the benefit of the general public, and particularly of domestic and rural consumers" with publicly and cooperatively owned electric power systems given preferential rights for the available electricity (16 USC 832c(a)).

The Administrator is authorized to "negotiate and enter into contracts for the sale at wholesale of electric energy, either for resale or direct consumption" (16 USC 832d(a)). Private persons or agencies (other than privately owned public utilities) are forbidden to resell this electric energy to a private utility. Contracts are to be for not more than twenty years, and are subject to rate adjustment not less frequently than once in five years. Pursuant to the preferential rights clause, a contract with a private utility can be cancelled upon 5 years' written notice if, in the judgment of the Administrator, there is reasonable likelihood that any part of the energy sold under the contract will be needed by a public entity. BPA's contracts must also contain stipulations concerning resale and resale rates to ensure that the ultimate consumer pays rates which are reasonable and nondiscriminatory.

Bonneville's rates are to be "established with a view to encouraging the widest possible diversified use of electric energy" (16 USC 832e). Rate schedules are prepared by the Administrator, subject to the approval of the Federal Power Commission (which may approve or reject any tendered proposal but may not itself initiate rate changes). The schedules are to be designed so as to permit the repayment of all construction costs allocated to power production (as opposed to other project purposes which may include navigation, flood control, irrigation or recreation) within 50 years of the commencement of operations. An interest component, set at 6-1/8 percent effective July 1, 1974, is also to be repaid to the federal treasury. To the extent that this interest rate understates the current cost of capital, federal power production is afforded a direct federal subsidy.

THE SOUTHWESTERN, SOUTHEASTERN, AND ALASKA POWER ADMINISTRATION

Multipurpose reservoir projects have been (and are) constructed and operated by the Army Corps of Engineers primarily for flood control and navigation. Hydroelectric power facilities were not a primary objective, but were installed to avoid wasting the use of falling water. The Secretary of the Army, under the requirements of the Flood Control Act of 1944 (16 USC 825(s)), releases any power which is not needed in the operation of the reservoir to the Secretary of the Interior who, in turn, is to dispose of it "in such manner as to encourage the most widespread use thereof at the lowest possible rates to consumers consistent with sound business principles . . ." The Southwestern Power Administration (SPA), Southeastern Power Administration (SEPA), and Alaska Power Administration (APA) were created by the Secretary of Interior to discharge this marketing function. As in the case of Bonneville, preference in the sale of hydroelectric energy must be given to public entities and cooperatives.

SPA, which was created in 1945, markets power in Missouri, Arkansas, Louisiana, Texas, Oklahoma, and Kansas from eighteen hydroelectric plants with an installed capacity of 1,712 Mw which generated 2.99 billion Kwh in 1972. Five projects are under construction. In fiscal year 1972 SPA sold 44 percent of its total energy to 41 cooperatives; 21 percent to 37 municipalities; 22 percent to five investor owned utilities; and 13 percent to four military installations, one federal bureau, one state owned utility and one aluminum company. SPA operates and maintains approximately 1,700 miles of high voltage transmission lines.

SEPA, which operates in a ten-state area and which was established in 1950, markets 1900 Mw of power from sixteen hydroelectric facilities (with six under construction) to 79 municipalities, 101 cooperatives, one state and one county agency, six privately owned utilities, and to TVA. The latter is the recipient of the power from the Cumberland Basin Project which represents 40 percent of SEPA's total installed capacity.

APA was created to market federal hydroelectric power in the state of Alaska and to discharge a regional planning function. In 1972 APA marketed 159,000 Kwh to three customers: 56 percent to the City of Anchorage and the remainder to two cooperatives.

The Secretary of the Interior is authorized by the 1944 Act, to build or acquire transmission lines when "necessary in order to make the power and energy generated at said projects available in wholesale quantities for sale on fair and reasonable terms. . . ." Present policy is to construct such facilities only if it is uneconomical to wheel power over privately owned lines or when private utilities refuse to undertake wheeling.

Electricity is to be marketed so as to encourage its most widespread use and is to be sold "at the lowest possible rates to consumers consistent with sound business principles" (16 USC 825(s)). However, rates are to be set to cover the costs associated with the production and transmission of power, and revenues are paid into the general federal treasury. The Federal Power Commission has the ability to influence the allocation of project costs to power production and must approve the rate schedules of each of the marketing agencies but cannot itself initiate rate modifications.

BUREAU OF RECLAMATION

The Bureau of Reclamation constructs, operates, and maintains water storage projects for the reclamation of arid and semiarid lands in the western states. If consistent with the primary purpose of irrigation, hydroelectric power is generated and marketed by the Bureau. Power is produced at 50 facilities in 17 continguous states west of the Mississippi River. The Bureau had an installed capacity of 7,622 Mw in 1972.

The mandate of Section 5 of the Flood Control Act of 1944 (16 USC 825s) to sell power at the "lowest possible rates to consumers consistent with sound business principles" applies also to power marketed from reclamation projects and preference is to be given to public entities and cooperatives. Rate schedules are to be designed so that the realized revenues will cover, in addition to an interest component, the cost of operation and maintenance of the power facilities.

The Secretary of the Interior may include other charges at his discretion; whether or not Federal Power Commission approval is required is dependent upon the specific legislation governing the individual reclamation project. No particular type or form of rate is dictated by law, and the Bureau has not adopted a standard schedule. Each of the Bureau's firm wholesale rate schedules includes a separate demand charge. Some schedules employ a block rate structure for the recovery of energy charges; only in one instance is use made of more than two blocks. The trend is toward a flat energy charge.

THE RURAL ELECTRIFICATION PROGRAM

In 1935 central station electric and telephone service was largely unavailable in rural America. The Rural Electrification Administration (REA) was created by executive order in an attempt to address the problem; it was followed by enactment of the Rural Electrification Act of 1936 (7 USC 901 *et seq.*). The Act continued the REA within the Department of Agriculture and set up a direct loan program to finance qualified cooperative associations for the purpose of providing generation, transmission and/or distribution of electric power to rural residents not receiving central station service. In 1944 a 2 percent interest rate and a 35-year maximum repayment schedule was prescribed for REA loans.

Agreeing to serve all would-be customers in their areas, rural cooperatives were able to organize and to provide low cost electricity as a result of the low interest loans. Today there are approximately 1,000 rural electric systems serving 25 million customers. The cooperatives are engaged primarily in distribution of power purchased from other sources. Rural cooperatives own 44 percent of all distribution lines in the United States but only approximately 1 percent of the country's generating capacity. Rural systems average 3.9 consumers and $850.00 gross annual revenue per mile of line (about 1/10 as many customers and 1/15 the revenue per mile of line of most investor owned utilities).

REA is essentially a source of finance. Under the original provisions of the 1936 Act, the Secretary of the Treasury was authorized and directed to make loans to the Administrator, upon request and approval of the Secretary of Agriculture, in such amounts as Congress would appropriate. The Administrator reviewed loan applications and approved or disapproved them based upon a showing of need, the adequacy of security, and the probability of repayment within a 35-year period. No loan could be made for construction, operation, or enlargement of cooperative generating facilities unless prior consent of state authorities was obtained.

Early in 1973 curtailment of the 2 percent direct loan program was announced by the Office of Management and Budget which proceeded to freeze appropriated funds. Ultimately new legislation was enacted providing for a 5 percent insured and guaranteed loan program with some direct 2 percent loans available for "hardship" cases (P.L. 93-32 93rd Cong.). Under the new law REA can also guarantee private loans. As a result of the changes, rural electric cooperatives must now rely heavily on private financing. As a result, Cooperative Finance Corporation, which was created for the purpose of borrowing in the commercial money market to provide supplemental funding for electric coopera-tives, will be an important source of funds.

Cooperatives are not subject to regulation by the Federal Power Commission.[a] They are, however, generally subject to state certification where such requirements exist. Rural electric cooperatives are nonprofit customer-owned associations. Any revenue in excess of capital costs is therefore patronage capital. While cooperatives seek to maintain customary equity, and to obtain sufficient revenues to repay loans (at low interest rates), they do not have any obligation to pay stockholder dividends based on regulated rate base formulas. In the past they have been able to provide power at relatively low retail rates, although the recent program changes, higher fuel costs, and inflation might necessitate significant rate increases.

Cooperatives represent the first major deviation from the total vertical integration which marks most utilities. In several instances, distribution cooperatives have joined together to form a separate generation and transmission (G&T) cooperative. The G & T in turn seeks to meet the long capacity needs of participating systems while maximizing the advantages of economies of scale. Rates of the G & T are controlled by the participants through memberships on its board of directors. The G & T is typically required to obtain 35-year full requirements contracts from the participants to serve as security for REA or private financing. The REA does have some ability to influence both the wholesale and retail rates of cooperative entities based primarily on its mandate to assure the economic integrity of the cooperative system and its authority to set conditions on the expenditures of loaned funds.

---

[a]See *Alabama Power Co. v. Alabama Elec. Co-op, Inc.*, 394 F.2d 672 (5th Circuit, 1965), and *City of Paris, Kentucky v. FPC*, 399 F.2d 983 (DC Circuit, 1968).

TENNESSEE VALLEY AUTHORITY

The Tennessee Valley Authority, an independent, federally owned corporation, was established in 1933 to facilitate the development of the Tennessee River system and other regional resources. TVA enjoys many of the powers inherent in a corporate form, and is managed by a board of three directors appointed by the President, with the advice and consent of the Senate. At present TVA supplies power from 29 dams and twelve steam plants which it operates, and from seven Corps of Engineers and twelve Aluminum Company of America dams to 160 local publicly owned systems serving approximately 2-1/3 million customers in seven states.

The power program is a self-supporting and self-liquidating operation, bearing all costs related to power supply. Operating expenses are financed from power revenues; construction costs are financed from both revenues and borrowings. The Act was amended in 1959 to authorize TVA to borrow funds through bonds, notes, and other evidences of indebtedness, the proceeds of which may be used only for power facilities; nonpower activities continue to be supported by appropriated funds. Unlike earlier bonds, the present issues are not obligations of, nor guaranteed by, the federal government. The Secretary of the Treasury must approve the time of issuance and the maximum rate of interest to be borne by the bonds.

Until the mid 1950s most of the money needed to finance construction of power facilities came from appropriations which had to be repaid to the federal treasury together with an annual federal dividend. Payments in lieu of taxes are paid to those states and local governments in which TVA has acquired properties that were previously subject to state and local taxation. Approximately $28 million was paid in 1972.

The production and sale of electricity is to be primarily for the benefit of domestic and rural customers. Marketing contracts are limited to 20-year terms. States, counties, municipalities, and cooperatives are preference customers. Contracts with private utilities must contain a provision enabling the board to cancel the contract upon five years' written notice if power is needed to supply the demands of preference customers. Sales to industry are expressly made a "secondary purpose" intended to obtain the advantages of high load factor sales and the resulting cost benefit for domestic and rural consumers.

Contracts between TVA and a public body must include provisions for the resale of electricity at rates which do not discriminate between consumers of the same class. Contracts with privately owned utilities must actually prescribe the resale rate schedules.

TVA sells power to preference customers pursuant to a two-part tariff consisting of a single demand charge and a separate energy charge, which declines in amount per kwh as consumption increases. Resale is pursuant to standard residential and commercial rate schedules established by TVA which, for the most part, are of the declining block rate type. Rates charged by TVA are comparatively low. In 1972 the average TVA homeowner paid 1.28¢ per kwh and used 14,040 kwh; the average homeowner in the United States, paid 2.25¢ per kwh and used 7,496 kwh.

The board is authorized to expand existing facilities and to construct new plants as needed. In the early 1950s, as its demand began to exceed the capacity of its hydroelectric facilities, TVA began to construct coal-fired steam plants. Today, approximately 80 percent of its generation is from steam plants and its dependence on strip-mined coal has been the subject of criticism and litigation by environmental organizations. TVA forcasts that its demand will approximately double in the next ten years. At present, it is involved in the largest construction program in its history with 16 million kilowatts of capacity under construction or on order—mostly nuclear units for base load and pumped storage and gas turbines for peaking.

Bibliography

Bibliography

A.B. Atkinson and L. Waverman, "Resource Allocation and the Regulated Firm: Comment," *Bell Journal of Economics and Management Science*, Spring 1973, *4*, 283-287.

Elizabeth E. Bailey, "Peak Load Pricing Under Regulatory Constraint," *Journal of Policital Economy*, July/August 1972, *80*, 662-679.

Elizabeth E. Bailey and John C. Malone, "Resource Allocation and the Regulated Firm," *Bell Journal of Economics and Management Science*, Spring 1970, *1*, 129-142.

Elizabeth E. Bailey, "Resource Allocation and the Regulated Firm: Comments on Comments," *Bell Journal of Economics and Management Science*, Spring 1973, *4*, 283-287.

William J. Baumol and David F. Bradford, "Optimal Departures From Marginal Cost Pricing," *American Economic Review*, June, 1970, *60*, 265-283.

J.G. Boggis, "Innovations in Domestic Tariff Metering: Time Tariffs," *Electricity* XIX, Sept.-Oct. 1966, 241-244.

Marcel Boiteux, "Peak-Load Pricing," *Journal of Business*, April 1960, *33*, 157-179.

P. Caillé, "Marginal Cost Pricing in a Random Future as Applied to the Tariff for Electrical Energy," *Electricité de France*, 99-120.

Eli W. Clemens, "Marginal Cost Pricing: A Comparison of French and American Industrial Power Rates," *Land Economics*, November 1964, 380-404.

Michael Crew and Paul Kieindorfer, "Marshall and Turvey on Peak Load or Joint Product Pricing," *Journal of Political Economy*, July/August 1971, *74*, 1369-1377.

Donald N. De Salvia, "An Application of Peak Load Pricing," *Journal of Business*, October 1969, *42*, 458-476.

Noel M. Edelson, "Resource Allocation and the Regulated Firm: A Reply to Bailey and Malone," *Bell Journal of Economics and Management Science*, Spring 1971, 2, 374-378.

G. Hadley, *Nonlinear and Dynamic Programming*, Palo Alto: Addison-Wesley, 1964.

H.S. Houthakker, Philip Verleger, Jr., and Dennis P. Sheehan, "Dynamic Demand Analyses for Gasoline and Residential Electricity," unpublished manuscript MIT.

Michael D. Intriligator, *Mathematical Optimization and Economic Theory*, Englewood Cliffs, N.J.: Prentice-Hall, 1971.

Stephen C. Littlechild, "Marginal-Cost Pricing with Joint Costs," *The Economic Journal*, June 1970, *LXXX*, 58-97.

Pierre Masse, "Some Economic Effects of the Tarif Vert," *Revue Francaise de l'Energie*, 97, May 1958, 392-395.

Ronald L. Meek, "An Application of Marginal Cost Pricing: The Green Tariff in Theory and Practice," *Journal of Industrial Economics*, July 1963, Part I: Theory, 217-236. Part II: Practice, November 1963, 45-63.

Stewart Meyers, "The Application of Finance Theory to Public Utility Rate Cases," *Bell Journal of Economics and Management Science*, Spring 1972, *3*, 58-97.

V. Kerry Smith, "The Implications of Regulation for Induced Technical Change," Forthcoming in *Bell Journal of Economics and Management Science*, 1974.

Ralph Turvey, "Peak-Load Pricing," *Journal of Political Economy*, January/February 1968, 76, 107-113.

Ralph Turvey, *Economic Analysis and Public Enterprises*, Totowa, N.J.: Rowman and Littlefield, 1971.

Ralph Turvey, *Optimal Pricing and Investment in Electricity Supply*, Cambridge, Massachusetts, MIT Press, 1968.

William S. Vickrey, "Responsive Pricing of Public Utility Services," *Bell Journal of Economics and Management Science*, Spring 1971, 2, 337-346.

William S. Vickrey, "Pricing and Resource Allocation in Transportation and Public Utilities," *American Economic Review*, 452-65.

Oliver E. Williamson, "Peak Load Pricing and Optimal Capacity Under Indivisibility Constraints," *American Economic Review*, September 1966, *56*, 810-827.

Reviewer Comment

National Association of Regulatory Utility Commissioners
Committee on
Electric and Nuclear Energy

Comments on "Perspective on Power:
A Study of the Regulation and Pricing
of Electric Power"

The authors' biases are apparent throughout. Particular examples of a theoretical rather than an experienced approach are apparent in the *Pricing* sections where non-typical load curves are. utilized. This may have led to the important variation in demand over the daily cycle being virtually ignored in concentrating recommendations on seasonal variations.

In overemphasizing the potential effect of price on demand all other rate-making considerations are entirely ignored. The role of cost allocation in rate design is dismissed as its use having been limited. No reference is made to the NARUC's 1973 Electric Utility Cost Allocation Manual. Cost criteria—for example, Long Run Incremental Costs (LRIC)—are only relied upon when they currently indicate higher rate levels. No reference is made to what rates would have resulted under these criteria in prior periods, e.g., in the 1960's where LRIC was much lower than average costs. The author's concepts on LRIC and elasticity will not stand the test of decreasing as well as increasing costs in meeting the apparent objectives.

The proposal for an *Inflation* adjustment suggests no regulatory constraints or responsible customer safeguards.

The Regulatory Framework includes no significant current analysis of State Commission regulation despite the fact that practically all of the electric utilities rate schedules are subject to State Commission rather than federal jurisdiction. *Reorganizing Regulation* through establishment of regional commissions rather than resolving certain issues nationally is recommended, presumably to provide regional options. No objective analysis is presented as to why state options should be eliminated. Emphasis on a more competitive industry structure placing greater reliance on the operation of market forces indicates some indifference to the concept of carefully regulated electric rates.

Restructuring the Electric Power Industry is based on the particular importance of inter-utility competition. No objective data is presented to support competitive operations. The industries' prior experience in competitive operations indicated higher costs from competing systems. Mergers have resulted in decreased costs, more efficient operations and elimination of duplicating facilities.

Index

ACRS (Advisory Committee on Reactor Safeguards), 84
Administrative Procedure Act, 101
A.E.C. (Atomic Energy Commission), 53, 83
air conditioning, xviii, 13
allocation, 22, 47
amortization accounts, 58
Anderson, K.P., 120
APA (Alaska Power Administration), 159
Arkansas, 65, 159
Army Corps of Engineers, 158
Averch, H. and Johnson, L.L., 146; A–J effect, 59

Bailey, E., 142; –and White, L.J., 142
Baumol, W.J., 146; –and Bradford, D.F., 130
blackout: 1965, 73, 92; syndrome, 56
block pricing, 155
Bonbright, T., 25
BPA (Bonneville Power Administration), 68, 157
Boone, C.C., 9
Bureau of Reclamation, 157–159

California, 157
capacity, 18, 41; costs, 22; –cost avoidance goal, 46
capital, 74; factor input, 3; growth, 91; –intensiveness, 153; rate base, 107
Cicchetti, C.J., 121
"coincidental peak method," 47
Colorado, 106
competition: intraindustry, 61
Con Ed, 10
Congress: interstate industry, 88; long-range needs, 93; preferential treatment, 68

construction, 2; growth projections, 90; incentive, 65
consumer demand, 125, 139
consumption, 14, 32, 117; discounts, 60; price elasticity, 86
contracts: BPA, 158
cooperatives, 161; –Finance Corp., 162
corporate abuses, 58
costs, 143; characteristics, 29; distribution, 36, 43; minimization, 18, 88; overruns, 5; transmission, 33
cross-subsidization, 36
Cumberland Basin Projects, 159

daily load cycle, 25
demand: average and excess, 48; component, 16; interdependence, 146; projections, 56
depreciation, 58
DeSalvia, H., 38
Detroit Edison, 66
discrimination, 15
disputes: rate payers, 42
distribution, 110; regulatory function, 108
Division of Reactor Licensing, 84
Doherty rates, 43

ECAR (East Central Area Reliability Coordination Agreement), 73
economies of scale, 2; block rate pricing, 46; and competition, 110; construction, 80; definition, 6; needs, 96; pooling, 75; small utility, 104
elasticity, 13; demand for power, 29; peak demand, 38
electricity: bulk power supply, 107; demand, 85–86; distribution, 94; his-

About the Authors

Edward Berlin did his undergraduate work at the College of the City of New York and received his Bachelor and Master of Laws Degrees from Columbia and Georgetown Universities respectively. After spending five years at the Justice Department doing civil appellate work he joined the Federal Power Commission where he served as Assistant General Counsel with responsibility for that agency's legislative program. In January, 1969 he left the government to form the law firm of Berlin, Roisman and Kessler which specializes in the representation of citizen groups with regard to environmental, consumer and employment discrimination matters. The firm represented the environmental groups in the landmark *Calvert Cliffs* case and Mr. Berlin has participated in the litigation over the Alaska Pipeline, Four Corners Power Plants, the use of DDT, the location of transmission lines including representation of citizens who secured a major change in the routing and location of facilities in a precedent setting decision by the Virginia State Corporation Commission. He has also been active, on behalf of the Environmental Defense Fund, in electric rate proceedings before the Michigan, New York, and Wisconsin Public Utility Commissions, in seeking to initiate commitments to peak load pricing. Mr. Berlin teaches environmental law and regulatory courses at the University of Denver Law School and at the Law School, Institute for Environmental Studies and College of Engineering of the University of Wisconsin.

Charles J. Cicchetti, an Associate Professor of Economics at the University of Wisconsin-Madison, received his undergraduate training at Colorado College and his Ph.D. from Rutgers. Between 1969 and 1972 he was with Resources for the Future in Washington, D.C. Dr. Cicchetti's work has focused primarily on the interaction between economics and environmental and energy matters. He has both published and lectured extensively on each of those subjects and is a frequent witness before Congressional Committees. Included among his prior books is an analysis of the economic implications of the Alaskan oil pipeline (*Alaskan Oil: An Economic and Environmental Analysis of Alternative Routes and Markets*, Johns Hopkins Press for Resources for the Future, 1972) and several works dealing with recreational demand forecasting. Dr. Cicchetti is a member of the American Economic Association Econometric Society, Royal Economic Society, American Association for the Advancement of Science and the Western Economic Association and serves on several Editorial and Advisory Boards including as a Director of the Public Interest Economics Center. Over the past year, Dr. Cicchetti has regularly appeared as an expert witness before state and federal agencies on the subject of electricity utility pricing and has served as a consultant to government agencies on that and related issues.

William J. Gillen did his undergraduate and graduate work in Economics at George Washington University. He has served on the staffs of the Environmental Law Institute, the Natural Resources Policy Center and the Environmental Defense Fund. His publications include analyses of the benefit-cost evaluation of federal watershed programs, the mandatory oil import program, and the full range of environmental and economic issues confronting the electric power industry. He has appeared as an expert witness on utility pricing matters before state and federal commissions and has served as a consultant to federal agencies.